BASIC
ENGLISH GRAMMAR

BASIC ENGLISH GRAMMAR

by Bonnie L. Walker

Media Materials, Inc.   Baltimore, Maryland

THE AUTHOR

Bonnie L. Walker has taught for sixteen years in junior and senior high schools and in college. She holds a Ph.D. degree in curriculum theory and educational media from the University of Maryland and has also earned a bachelor's of arts degree with honors in English. She studied psycholinguistics at the University of Illinois Graduate School. She is the author of several workbooks, learning packages, and sound filmstrips in written expression, grammar, and usage.

Editor: Barbara Pokrinchak, Ed.D.
Editorial Consultant: M. E. Criste

Printed in the United States of America.

09 86 VG   5.0

ISBN: 0-86601-061-0

CONTENTS

Acknowledgments

The author wishes to thank the many teachers, students, and administrators whose advice guided the development of the text, and to express her appreciation to her husband, Bill, and to her daughter, April, for their encouragement and many helpful suggestions.

Preface

    Basic English Grammar is designed to help secondary students and adults to master the skills needed to use standard English effectively. The simple sentence structure and low-level vocabulary used in the text should lead to comprehension without frustration. The content of the activities is meant to appeal to the interests of students. Each topic is carefully subdivided so that only one rule or concept is presented at a time and is accompanied by at least one practice exercise.

    The textbook was developed after a series of interviews with teachers, supervisors, and students themselves. Members of all of these groups voiced a pressing need for a textbook which would (1) present rules and concepts one at a time, and (2) provide opportunities for appropriate practice. *Basic English Grammar* seeks to accommodate both these objectives, utilizing a clear approach which will be appealing and effective for students.

ORGANIZATION OF THE TEXT

    The book is organized into Chapters, Lessons, and Activities. All chapters begin with an overview of the topic and Chapter Warm-Ups, which may be used as diagnostic activities or pretests. Each lesson focuses on the development of one important subtopic or concept related to the main idea. Within each lesson the rules are presented with accompanying activities. Grammar and usage are presented together in each lesson to facilitate the understanding of rules and their practical application to the patterns of written and spoken English. Review activities are incorporated within lessons and at the end of chapters.

TEACHER'S GUIDE

Information about the readability of *Basic English Grammar* is provided in the *Teacher's Guide and Answer Key* which accompanies the textbook. Since a low-level vocabulary was essential in the content of the activities, the author made frequent reference to *A Revised Core Vocabulary*, by S. E. Taylor, H. Frackenpohl, and C. E. White, New York: EDL/McGraw-Hill, 1979. Words were carefully selected to present the rules as clearly as possible without talking down to students and to make the topics in the activities as relevant as possible.

The Teacher's Guide also contains for each lesson a summary, objectives, a vocabulary list, teaching suggestions, follow-up activities, and answers to all exercises. There is a supplementary, reproducible worksheet for each chapter.

PART ONE:

GRAMMAR AND USAGE

What Is Grammar?

> Grammar is the study of language. When we study grammar, we are studying the rules of our language. We follow these rules when we speak and when we write. The purpose of grammar is to help us communicate our ideas effectively.

The activities in this introductory section will help you understand what grammar is and what the study of language includes.

■ **Grammar includes the way words are arranged in a sentence.**

ACTIVITY 1. Here are some groups of words which do not make sense. Rearrange the words on your paper so that they have meaning.

1. Graduated from high school in June Jack.
2. Went Howard on a vacation.
3. To a new band listened Mike.

ACTIVITY 2. Decide whether these sentences are questions or statements. Add the correct end punctuation.

1. Do you want something to eat
2. Jack stopped at the store and bought sodas
3. Is Cathy going to the beach this summer

■ **Grammar also includes the rules for spelling, punctuation, and capitalization.**

When we talk, we use pauses and gestures to make our meaning clear. We also emphasize some words more than others. We can talk in a loud or soft voice. When we write, however, we use punctuation and capitalization to help us make our meaning clear. Just as we pronounce words in the same way every time, we also spell them in a certain way.

ACTIVITY 3. Each of these sentences has a mistake. The mistake may be spelling, capitalization, or punctuation. Find the mistakes. Copy the sentences correctly on your own paper.
1. Andy lookd out of the window.
2. "Is this a good day for fishing," he wondered.
3. Last wednesday he caught several fish.
4. he caught an enormous catfish.
5. Andy decided to ask his friend joe.
6. He new they would have a good time.

■ **Grammar also includes rules about usage.**

The study of grammar includes the way we use words in sentences. When we write, we must express complete ideas. The subject and verb must agree. We must use the correct pronoun. Often we know when we hear a mistake in usage even when we do not know the exact rule.

ACTIVITY 4. Read each sentence. Find the usage mistake. Then write the sentence correctly.
1. Me and Charlie enjoy going to concerts.
2. Jackie and Fred have already went to the movies.
3. He changed the oil in his car hisself.
4. Gail don't like to eat spinach.
5. Us boys are going to play softball tonight.
6. That story doesn't make no sense.
7. Howard walked up to me and gives me an apple.

PARTS OF SPEECH

The English language has thousands of words. All of these words can be put into eight main groups. These groups are called parts of speech and are important for you to know. You can use your language better if you understand its grammar.

Nouns — Words that name people, places, things, and ideas.
Ted and his *girlfriend* enjoy *concerts.*

Pronouns — Words that replace nouns.
Everyone likes *him* very much.

Adjectives — Words that describe anyone or anything.
The last concert was *expensive.*

Verbs — Words that express action or a state of being in a sentence.
Ted *looked* at used cars all day.
My knee *is* hurt.

Adverbs — Words that tell about the action. They can tell how, when, where, or how much.
He drove his new car *carefully.*

Prepositions — Words which show relationships between a noun and the rest of the sentence.
Jack drove *over* the bumpy road.

Conjunctions — Words that connect sentences or parts of a sentence.
Bill *and* Ann bought the tickets.

Interjections — Words that express feelings.
Ouch! You stepped on my foot.

In this book you will study all eight parts of speech. You will understand your language better. Then it will be easier to use your language when you speak and when you write.

Every word in a sentence is a certain part of speech. Many words can be more than one part of speech. You must see the word in a sentence to know how it is used. For example, many words can be either nouns or adjectives.

Noun — I like to play *softball.*
Adjective — We went to a *softball* game.

A word can also be used as either a noun or a verb. You must read the sentence to be sure. A word that names someone or something is a noun. A word that expresses the action is a verb.

Verb — They *race* their cars every weekend.
Noun — The *race* started at three o'clock.

ACTIVITY 5. Read each sentence. What part of speech is the underlined word? Use the definitions and examples on page 4. Write your answer on your own paper.

1. Billy McGregor is a baseball player.
2. He enjoys playing baseball very much.
3. Billy plays second base.
4. He is a good hitter and fielder.
5. Billy is unusually quick.
6. After high school he tried out for a team.
7. Billy plays on a minor league team.
8. His batting average is 363.
9. Yeah, Billy! We wish you luck!

Chapter 1

Nouns—Words That Name Anyone or Anything

> Almost everything and everyone in the world has a name. We need to name things and people so that we can talk about them. Many things have more than one name. The words we use to name people and things are called *nouns*. A word is a noun when it names something or someone in a sentence. Nouns are words that name people, places, things, and ideas.

■ **A noun is a word that names someone or something.**

Before you begin the lessons in this chapter, do the Warm-Ups. They will help you find out how well you understand this part of speech.

WARM-UP 1. Find twenty nouns in these sentences. List them in order on your paper.
1. Ted is a student.
2. Last year Ted got a part-time job.
3. He saved his money and bought a used car.
4. His state requires owners to buy insurance.
5. Ted went to an insurance agent.
6. He had to make several decisions.
7. The agent sold him a policy.
8. The cost was high, but Ted got full coverage.
9. He wanted protection for his new car.

WARM-UP 2. Look at the picture below. Make a list of twenty or more nouns. Remember that nouns are words that name, people, places, things, and ideas. For example, the *smile* on the man's face is a noun. *Face* is also a noun.

Here are some nouns to get your list started:

wall   corner   picture   frame   tie   arm

Now you are ready to begin Lesson One.

LESSON ONE. FINDING NOUNS IN SENTENCES

> A *noun* is a word that names someone or something in a sentence. Read the examples:
>
> **Persons** — The insurance *agent* sold *Ted* a policy.
>
> **Places** — Most *states* require car owners to have insurance.
>
> **Things** — Ted saved his *money* and bought a *car.*
>
> **Amounts** — The *cost* was high, but Ted got full *coverage.*
>
> **Acts** or **Actions** — Ted had to make a decision.
>
> **Qualities** or **Characteristics** — The athlete had much courage.

ACTIVITY 1. Think of ten nouns that belong in each group. Some examples are given in parentheses. Write the lists on your paper.

1. time (day, second)
2. places (garage, city)
3. things (book, coat)
4. amounts (size, liter)
5. feelings (joy, fear)
6. events (concert, party)
7. persons (student, man)
8. actions (race, trip)
9. qualities (honesty, trust)

■ **A noun may be the name of a part of something.**

ACTIVITY 2. The words that name the parts of people or things are also nouns. Here is a list of nouns. Name five parts of each thing. Use the example below as a guide.

house — *room,   roof,   window,   garage,   wall*

1. stereo
2. car
3. television
4. bicycle
5. ship
6. tree

■ A noun may also be the name of a group of people, places, and things.

Groups of people	— group, audience, crowd
Groups of places	— United States, nation
Groups of things or animals	— herd, flock, collection

ACTIVITY 3. Read the sentences below. Find five nouns which name a group of things or people. List the words on your paper.
1. The baseball team practiced every day.
2. Ted's club had a meeting every Thursday.
3. The whole neighborhood went to the picnic.
4. Carla decided to join the navy.
5. The jury found the man innocent.

■ A compound word may also be a noun.

A compound word is two words joined together.
fire + fighter = *firefighter*   book + case = *bookcase*

ACTIVITY 4. Write a sentence using each of these compound nouns. Underline *all* of the nouns in your sentences.

1. sunflower
2. blindfold
3. earthquake
4. moonlight
5. thunderstorm
6. walkout
7. toothpaste
8. warehouse
9. watermelon
10. bookstore

■ A group of words may be a noun.

A group of words may be the name of something or someone. Sometimes the words are separate. Sometimes they have hyphens (-). Here are some examples.

White House	son-in-law	ice cream
Dr. Ed Tyler	Main Street	Secretary of State

ACTIVITY 5. Find all of the nouns in these sentences. Make a list of them on your paper.

1. A forget-me-not is a lovely blue flower.
2. The vice-president spoke at our graduation.
3. Mount McKinley National Park is in Alaska.
4. Jane was the maid-of-honor at the wedding.
5. Kim took her toothbrush and toothpaste on the trip.

■ **Nouns may be abstract or concrete.**

A *concrete* noun is a word that names something you can see or touch.

An *abstract* noun is a word that names something you can think about or talk about. You can't see it or touch it. An abstract noun is an idea.

Concrete Nouns	Abstract Nouns
money	cost
clock	time
school	education
steel	strength

ACTIVITY 6. Read each pair of words. On your paper, write the abstract noun in each pair.

1. fever thermometer
2. law judge
3. price price tag
4. fire emergency
5. pizza hunger
6. acrobat excitement
7. year calendar
8. love ring
9. earthquake disaster
10. Ted Jones courage

ACTIVITY 7. Find twenty nouns in the sentences below. List them on your paper in order.

1. When Ted Jones came home from his job, he was hungry.
2. He went to the refrigerator and opened the door.
3. Ted got three apples and a bottle of milk.
4. He got a glass from the cabinet.
5. He flipped on the TV and sat in his favorite chair.
6. His sister Janet came into the room.
7. "When do I get a ride in your new car?" Janet asked.
8. "In the next lesson!" he laughed.

LESSON REVIEW. Make a list of all of the nouns in these sentences.

1. Ted Jones wanted very much to buy a car.
2. Every week he saved a certain amount of money.
3. He put his money in a bank and received interest.
4. Finally, he made a decision to buy a car.
5. He wanted a small car that would get good gas mileage.
6. Ted saw an ad in the newspaper.
7. He called the phone number and made an appointment.
8. Ted looked at nine automobiles in two weeks.
9. Then he found the perfect car. The price was right!
10. Ted had a good feeling. He made the purchase!

LESSON TWO. NOUNS THAT ARE CAPITALIZED

A *common noun* is the name of a general type of person, place, thing, or idea.

A *proper noun* is the name of a particular person, place, thing, or idea.

Common Nouns	Proper Nouns
president	George Washington
athlete	Babe Ruth
race horse	Bold Venture
book	*Robinson Crusoe*
author	Pearl S. Buck
place	Alaska
day	Tuesday
document	the Constitution
movie	*Reds*

In this lesson you will study the difference between common and proper nouns. A common noun is capitalized only if it is the first word of a sentence or part of a title. A proper noun is always capitalized. See the examples in the box above.

ACTIVITY 1. Copy this list of common nouns on your paper. Write a proper noun beside each common noun. Do yours like this example:

actress — *Kate Jackson*

1. teacher
2. city
3. country
4. dog
5. actor
6. planet
7. president
8. river
9. baseball player
10. football team
11. newspaper
12. neighbor
13. singer
14. street
15. band
16. movie
17. holiday
18. month
19. high school
20. television show

ACTIVITY 2. Copy this list of words. Capitalize the words which are *proper nouns*. A proper noun names a particular person, place, thing, or idea.

1. school	8. july	15. john wayne
2. actor	9. mars	16. christmas
3. florida	10. england	17. mr. wilson
4. ocean	11. lassie	18. carpenter
5. park	12. road	19. california
6. china	13. america	20. wednesday
7. lake	14. paper	21. "chips"

ACTIVITY 3. Copy this list of proper nouns. Write a common noun after each. Do yours like these examples.

Joe Louis — *boxer* or *champion*
Canada — *country* or *place*

1. Boston	11. Baltimore
2. Warren Beatty	12. Atlantic Ocean
3. Hank Aaron	13. French
4. Fourth of July	14. Tom Sawyer
5. *Star Wars*	15. Bugs Bunny
6. Lassie	16. Venus
7. Mercedes Benz	17. Thanksgiving
8. The Beatles	18. the World Series
9. Ohio	19. Italy
10. Harvard	20. Florence Nightingale

ACTIVITY 4. Copy these sentences. Capitalize the proper nouns.

1. Last summer we drove to utah and saw the great salt lake.
2. A ruby is the birthstone for people born in july.
3. The author of *the sea wolf* was jack london.
4. The capital of austria is vienna.
5. In his last game, babe ruth hit three consecutive home runs.

■ **The name of a particular place is a proper noun.**

The name of a country, state, city, street, or building is a proper noun. Look at the examples below.

Common Nouns	Proper Nouns
city	New York City, Kansas City
river	the Mississippi River
street	Main Street
apartment	Apartment 103
route	Route 5 or Rte. 5
high school	Montgomery High School
park	Rock Creek Park

ACTIVITY 5. Copy each of the following sentences. Capitalize the proper nouns. Every sentence will have at least one proper noun.

1. Robert mailed a package to houston, texas.
2. His friend lives at 602 river drive, apartment 119.
3. Last year robert went to a new high school.
4. He liked northview senior high very much.
5. Robert and sue went fishing in the lake.
6. The lake was at the end of north shore drive.

■ **An abbreviation is a short form of a word. If the whole word is a proper noun, you capitalize the abbreviation.** Read the examples below.

Proper Noun	Abbreviation
Maryland	Md.
Doctor Smith	Dr. John Smith
Main Street	Main St.

ACTIVITY 6. Most of the words in an address are proper nouns. Write each of these addresses on your paper. Capitalize all of the proper nouns.

1. mr. joe keller
   route 2, box 206
   marshall, iowa 50152

2. mr. c. j. simmons
   1580 eton way
   burke, virginia 22015

■ **Parts of the country are proper nouns. Directions are common nouns.** Read the examples below.

Part of the country— I visited the *South* last spring.
Direction   — I am going *south* next spring.

ACTIVITY 7. Copy these sentences on your paper. Capitalize the proper nouns. Not every sentence will have a proper noun.

1. When ted graduated from high school, he took a trip to the south.
2. On the first day, he drove 300 miles southwest.
3. He started in baltimore and spent the first night in north carolina.
4. On the second day, ted drove west to visit some friends in tennessee.
5. The next day ted headed southeast to florida.

■ **The name of a language and a particular course** proper nouns. **The name of a subject is a comm** noun. Read the examples below.

Proper Nouns	Common Nouns
English, French	language
History I	social studies, ma

ACTIVITY 8. Read each pair of sentences. Copy sentence with correct capitalization.

1. A Karl got an A in English.
   B Karl got an A in english.
2. A Next year Ted is taking math and social st
   B Next year Ted is taking Math and Social St
3. A Janet signed up for math I.
   B Janet signed up for Math I.
4. A Carol enjoys physical education.
   B Carol enjoys Physical Education.

■ **A title is a proper noun. Books, songs, movies, and people are some of the things that can have a title. The first word and all main words in a title are capitalized.** Look at the examples below.

Reverend Frank Garcia   *Lord of the Rings*
"The Star Spangled Banner"   *The Red Pony*

ACTIVITY 9. Copy each of these titles on your own paper. Capitalize the first word and all important words.

1. *the red badge of courage*
2. *the sound of music*
3. *a man for all seasons*
4. "*you've got a friend*"
5. *the tonight show*
6. *the world almanac*
7. president andrew jackson
8. father james murphy

ACTIVITY 10. Copy each of these sentences on your own paper. Capitalize all of the proper nouns.

1. On wednesday ted came home from florida.
2. His sister janet was watching television.
3. "Hello, ted," janet said. "Welcome home from the south."
4. "Your boss, mr. jackson, called you yesterday," janet told him.
5. "He wants you to report to the office on mill stream drive tomorrow."
6. "Thanks," ted said. "Why are you home? I thought you were taking a french class."
7. "The class meets in the morning. How about taking me for the ride you promised? I'd like to go south myself."
8. "OK," ted agreed. "Let's go."

LESSON REVIEW. Copy the sentence in each pair that has correct capitalization.

1. A Ted and his sister drove down Rockledge drive.
   B Ted and his sister drove down Rockledge Drive.

2. A Rockledge Drive took them to the south part of town.
   B Rockledge drive took them to the South part of town.

3. A Janet talked about her french class.
   B Janet talked about her French class.

4. A Ted wanted to talk about the local football team.
   B Ted wanted to talk about the local Football Team.

5. A "Tell me about florida," Janet interrupted.
   B "Tell me about Florida," Janet interrupted.

6. A "I liked the Everglades national park," he said.
   B "I liked the Everglades National Park," he said.

7. A "Did you see any Alligators?"
   B "Did you see any alligators?"

8. A "Yes. I brought you a book about the Park."
   B "Yes. I brought you a book about the park."

9. A "Did you visit our friends, Mr. and Mrs. Sayers?"
   B "Did you visit our friends, mr. and mrs. sayers?"

10. A Ted turned onto route 50.
    B Ted turned onto Route 50.

11. A They drove past Wilson high school.
    B They drove past Wilson High School.

12. A "The south was nice, but it's good to be home," Ted said.
    B "The South was nice, but it's good to be home," Ted said.

LESSON THREE. SINGULAR AND PLURAL NOUNS

> A singular noun is the name of one person, place, thing, or idea.
>
> A plural noun is the name of more than one person, place, thing, or idea.
>
> The name of a group can be singular or plural.
>
> | Singular Nouns | Plural Nouns |
> |---|---|
> | singer | singers |
> | park | parks |
> | house | houses |
> | group | groups |

ACTIVITY 1. Make two lists with these words. Name one list *Singular*. Name the second list *Plural*.

1. action
2. feet
3. bunches
4. doctor
5. team
6. Ted
7. Main Street
8. nations
9. address
10. reports
11. summer
12. forest
13. bosses
14. majority
15. men
16. agents
17. towns
18. committee
19. circus
20. crowds

ACTIVITY 2. Copy each of these sentences. Decide whether the underlined noun is singular or plural. Do yours like the example.

The baseball *team* practiced every day. — singular

1. Fred tuned the *piano* yesterday.
2. She wrote the *sentences* carefully.
3. The *band* played in the park.
4. Play your new *record* for me.
5. We walked along the rough *path.*
6. Our *feet* became very sore.

■ **Most plural nouns end in -s or -es.** Read the examples.

Singular Nouns	Plural Nouns
ship	ships
group	groups
path	paths
church	churches
dish	dishes
six	sixes

When the plural noun ends in -es, the plural has an extra syllable. You can hear the difference if you say the words aloud.

ACTIVITY 3. Make each of these singular nouns plural. Add either an -s or -es. Say the plural aloud. You will hear the extra syllable when the plural noun ends in -es. Do yours like the examples:

town — *towns* **guess** — *guesses*

1. bunch
2. address
3. car
4. fox
5. book
6. patch
7. bench
8. school
9. ladder
10. mountain
11. ax
12. watch
13. team
14. river
15. wish
16. witch
17. idea
18. tax
19. sled
20. icicle
21. quiz

ACTIVITY 4. Each of the nouns in the list below is singular. Make the noun plural by adding an -s or -es. Then, use each plural noun in a sentence on your paper.

1. kiss
2. box
3. film
4. radio
5. beach
6. flash
7. tree
8. mess
9. batch
10. roof

■ Some nouns that end in -y become plural by changing the -y to -i and adding -es.

■ Some nouns that end in -y simply add an -s to become plural.

Look closely at the two lists below. Try to discover which nouns follow each rule.

Nouns That Change		Nouns That Do Not Change	
city	cities	key	keys
lady	ladies	alley	alleys
spy	spies	boy	boys

■ This is the difference:

The letter before the -y in *key*, *alley*, and *boy* is a vowel. These nouns become plural by adding an -s.

The letter before the -y in *city*, *lady*, and *spy* is a consonant. These nouns become plural by changing the -y to -i and adding -es.

ACTIVITY 5. Copy the list of nouns below. Make each noun plural. Do yours like these examples:

turkey — *turkeys*   **county** — *counties*

1. monkey
2. chimney
3. country
4. body
5. journey

6. injury
7. army
8. navy
9. bay
10. day

ACTIVITY 6. You will find five spelling mistakes in these sentences. Write the sentences correctly.

1. The spys from the two countrys were both ladys.
2. The men's bodys were completely covered with soot after they cleaned the chimneys.
3. Those boys fell and received many injurys.

■ The plural of most nouns that end in -f or -fe is made by adding -s.

roof, roofs   chief, chiefs

■ Some nouns that end in -f or -fe change the -f to -v and add -s or -es.

leaf, leaves   calf, calves

■ The plural of some nouns ending with a consonant and an -o is formed by adding -es.

hero, heroes   tomato, tomatoes

■ A few nouns become plural by changing letters within the word.

man, men   foot, feet   mouse, mice
woman, women   tooth, teeth   goose, geese

■ Some singular and plural nouns are spelled the same.

deer   sheep   trout   series

ACTIVITY 7. Find the spelling mistakes in these sentences. Write the sentences correctly.
1. Last winter the mans shot two deers.
2. The rancher bought eighty sheeps.
3. We went fishing and caught seven trouts.
4. The Reds won two World Serieses in a row.
5. They ate six loafs of bread and ten potatos.

ACTIVITY 8. Write the plural of each of these singular nouns. Then use the plural in a sentence.

goose-geese. The geese honked as they flew.

1. calf
2. belief
3. foot
4. man
5. tooth
6. foreman
7. team
8. knife
9. lady
10. monkey
11. tomato
12. potato
13. mouse
14. hero
15. deer

LESSON REVIEW

Part 1. Find 26 nouns in the sentences below. List them on your paper in order.

1. Ted and Janet decided to have a party.
2. In one week, Janet would go back to school.
3. Ted was taking courses at the community college.
4. This party would celebrate the beginning of a new year.
5. Janet shopped for sodas, potato chips, and other snacks.
6. Ted cleaned the house and got the records ready.
7. Their parents promised to stay in the TV room.
8. The time came soon and their friends arrived.
9. With so much preparation, the party would be a success.

Part 2. Read the following paragraph. Find six plural nouns. List them on your paper in order.

The traffic in front of the house was heavy for about two hours. About twenty people came to the party. Everyone seemed to be wearing new clothes. The guests stood in small groups around the snacks and around the stereo. They talked about their summer fun and the year to come.

Part 3. Write the plural of each of these nouns.

1. woman	8. spy	15. address
2. sheep	9. child	16. deer
3. goose	10. city	17. path
4. tomato	11. tax	18. agent
5. life	12. policy	19. party
6. hero	13. dish	20. knife
7. key	14. potato	21. trout

LESSON FOUR. NOUNS THAT ARE POSSESSIVE

> A noun that is possessive shows ownership or a relationship. A possessive noun has an apostrophe ('). Look at the examples.
>
> **Ownership** — That car belongs to Ted.
> That is *Ted's* car.
>
> **Relationship**— Janet is the sister of Ted.
> Janet is *Ted's* sister.

Remember that most plural nouns end in -*s* or -*es*. A noun that is possessive also ends in -*s*. Plurals and possessive nouns sound the same when they are said aloud. Many people get plurals and possessives mixed up when they write them. A written possessive noun looks different from a plural noun. Look at the examples below. Say the words aloud. Notice the difference in the meaning.

Plural Noun	**Possessive Noun**
We bought two *records*.	The *record's* cover is lost.

ACTIVITY 1. Find the underlined word in each sentence. Decide if the word is a plural or a possessive. Write the word. Then write the word *plural* or *possessive* after it. Do yours like this example:

Chicago has some of the world's tallest buildings.

world's — *possessive*

1. Ted's insurance policy came in the mail.
2. The policy had several pages.
3. A few of Ted's friends stopped by the house.
4. They came to see their friend's new car.
5. They went out to inspect the car's tires.
6. The tires were brand new.

■ **A possessive noun can be singular or plural.**
Read the rules and study the examples below.

Rule One

Make a singular noun possessive by adding -'s.

Singular	Singular Possessive
teacher	*teacher's* desk
child	*child's* bike

Rule Two

Make a plural noun that ends in -s possessive by adding only an apostrophe (').

Plural	Plural Possessive
teachers	*teachers'* meeting
trees	*trees'* leaves

Rule Three

When a plural noun does not end in -s, make it possessive by adding -'s.

Plural	Plural Possessive
men	*men's* department
children	*children's* room

ACTIVITY 2. Find the possessive nouns in these sentences. Write them on your paper. Write *singular* or *plural* after each word. Do yours like this example:

The ladies' department had a sale.   **ladies'** — *plural*

1. The albums' covers were all lost.
2. The cat slept on the sofa's cushion.
3. Ted had to replace the television's picture tube.
4. The mice's tracks led under the baseboard.
5. Last week the children's room was painted.

ACTIVITY 3. Here is a list of nouns. Write the singular and plural possessive form for each word. Do yours like these examples:

| club | — | *club's* | *clubs'* |
| lady | — | *lady's* | *ladies'* |

1. chapter	11. fox		
2. job	12. wife		
3. agent	13. child		
4. thing	14. man		
5. person	15. church		
6. noun	16. foot		
7. state	17. crowd		
8. goose	18. sunflower		
9. president	19. navy		
10. audience	20. monkey		

■ **Use an apostrophe in phrases such as** *one dollar's worth* **or** *week's vacation.* **If the word is plural and ends in -s, just add an apostrophe.**

Singular Nouns	**Plural Nouns**
one *dollar's* worth	two *dollars'* worth
a *week's* vacation	two *weeks'* vacation

ACTIVITY 4. Read each pair of sentences. Copy the correct sentence in each pair on your paper.

1. a Fred likes to put in his two cents' worth.
   b Fred likes to put in his two cent's worth.
2. a Ted got one weeks vacation every year.
   b Ted got one week's vacation every year.
3. a You will only have a minutes' wait.
   b You will only have a minute's wait.
4. a I'd like four dollar's worth of stamps.
   b I'd like four dollars' worth of stamps.
5. a We hoped for a rest at the week's end.
   b We hoped for a rest at the weeks end.

LESSON REVIEW

Part 1. Make a list of the possessive nouns in these sentences. Add apostrophes where they are needed.

1. Teds job is very important to him.
2. He has worked in Mr. Jacksons store for one year.
3. Mr. Jackson sells mens sports clothes.
4. Every week at the salespersons meeting they talk about their work.
5. Mr. Jacksons plan is to make Ted a manager some day.

Part 2. In the sentences below, some of the nouns are underlined. Make a list of these nouns. Identify each one as a plural noun or a possessive noun. Add an apostrophe if it is needed.

Several <u>years</u> ago, Janet and Ted went to New York.

years — *plural noun*

1. Janet and Ted went to New York City with their <u>parents.</u>
2. They wanted to see the <u>worlds</u> tallest buildings.
3. <u>Teds</u> favorite place was the Statue of Liberty.
4. One of the <u>familys</u> most enjoyable places was Lincoln Center.
5. Janet and her mother shopped for <u>womens</u> clothes.
6. Ted and his father went to Madison Square Garden to see some boxing <u>matches.</u>
7. The <u>crowds</u> of people and the <u>subways</u> were exciting.
8. At the <u>trips</u> end they all hoped to go again soon.

CHAPTER REVIEW

Part 1. Make a list of all of the nouns in these sentences. Include possessive nouns in your list.

1. The party was over.
2. Ted and Janet let their parents out of the TV room.
3. Mrs. Jones looked at the living room.
4. Records, glasses, and empty bowls were everywhere.
5. Ted and Janet cleaned up their friends' mess.
6. It was the end of a great evening.

Part 2. Only the first word in these sentences is capitalized. Find all of the proper nouns and write them on your paper. Capitalize them.

1. The summer was almost over. In august janet and ted would both return to school.
2. Janet was going to be a senior at wilson high school.
3. Ted was going to the hanover community college.
4. He also planned to work part-time at mr. jackson's store.
5. Janet was taking french, math, and science.
6. Ted was taking english and business subjects.
7. Ted remembered his trip to the south.
8. When his english teacher asked him to write a composition, he had a good topic.
9. He decided to title his paper "my first trip to florida."

Part 3. Write the plural form of each of these singular nouns.

1. wolf
2. city
3. quiz
4. teacher
5. student
6. monkey
7. house
8. party
9. child
10. tooth

Part 4. Read each pair of sentences. Which one is correct? Copy the correct sentence on your paper.

1. Ted and his friend andy went to the movies.
   Ted and his friend Andy went to the movies.

2. They were seeing *star wars* for the fifth time.
   They were seeing *Star Wars* for the fifth time.

3. The theater had special prices on wednesday.
   The theater had special prices on Wednesday.

4. They were going to the Early Show.
   They were going to the early show.

5. Ted had to study for an english test.
   Ted had to study for an English test.

6. Andy also went to hanover community college.
   Andy also went to Hanover Community College.

7. Andy was taking Basic Computers I.
   Andy was taking basic computers I.

8. He planned to become a computer operator.
   He planned to become a Computer Operator.

9. On the way home there was a lot of traffic.
   On the way home there was a lot of traffics.

10. Ted and Andy talked about their colleges team.
    Ted and Andy talked about their college's team.

11. They wondered about the teams' chances.
    They wondered about the team's chances.

12. When they got home, Teds sister was waiting.
    When they got home, Ted's sister was waiting.

13. Andy had been one of Janet's heros for years.
    Andy had been one of Janet's heroes for years.

14. "Did you get your dollar's worth?" Janet asked.
    "Did you get your dollars worth?" Janet asked.

15. "Yes. It is the worlds best show!" he said.
    "Yes. It is the world's best show!" he said.

2

Pronouns—Words That Replace Nouns

> When we speak or write, we identify the person or thing we are talking about. The word we use to name the person or thing is a noun. After we have said or written the name, we may use another part of speech to refer to the person or thing. The part of speech that we use is a *pronoun*.

■ **A pronoun is a word used instead of a noun.**

John is a senior. <u>He</u> is on the track team.

In this chapter you will study different kinds of pronouns. Before you begin the lessons, do the Warm-Ups. You will find out how well you understand pronouns.

WARM-UP 1. Find six pronouns in these sentences. List them in order on your paper.

1. Janet looked for her new homeroom.
2. She walked up the stairs to the third floor.
3. Janet found an old friend. They were in the same homeroom.
4. "That must be the place," said Janet.
5. "Lucky us!" laughed Darleen.
6. "At least we won't be late the first day!"

■ **The noun that the pronoun replaces is called the antecedent.**

Janet is a student. <u>She</u> is a senior.

Pronoun — She   **Antecedent** — Janet

WARM-UP 2. The pronoun in each of these sentences is underlined. List each pronoun on your paper. Then write the noun that the pronoun has replaced. Do your work like the example above.

1. Darleen and Janet are both seniors. <u>They</u> are old friends.
2. Ms. Lambert is the homeroom teacher. <u>She</u> also teaches French.
3. James Melcher is in the class. Janet has known <u>him</u> for years.
4. "How about a phone number?" James asked Janet. "Here <u>it</u> is," Janet said.
5. "Please call <u>me</u> this evening," Janet said.

WARM-UP 3. Read these sentences. Choose the correct pronoun in parentheses. Write the whole sentence on your paper. Underline the pronoun. Do yours like this example:

Darleen and Janet found <u>their</u> homeroom. (their, her)

1. Darleen and _____ are in the same French class. (I, me)
2. Please walk _____ girls to class. (we, us)
3. _____ room is yours? (Which, What)
4. Everyone is trying to find _____ first period class. (his, their)
5. James went to his class by _____ . (hisself, himself)

Now you are ready to begin Lesson One.

LESSON ONE. PERSONAL PRONOUNS

A pronoun is a word that replaces a noun. Without pronouns we would have to repeat the same nouns over and over again. Read the example:

Janet said that *Janet* was going to call *Janet's* mother.

Janet said that <u>she</u> was going to call <u>her</u> mother.

Remember that every pronoun has an antecedent. The antecedent is the noun that the pronoun replaces. The pronoun must agree with the antecedent in person, case, number, and gender.

Janet is going to call her mother.
She is leaving now.

Janet is the antecedent for the pronoun *she*.

There are several kinds of pronouns. The first kind that you will study is the personal pronoun.

■ **A personal pronoun is one that distinguishes the speaker, the person spoken to, and the person or thing spoken about.** Read these examples:

The first person is the speaker. *I* am late.
The second person is the person spoken to.
      You are late.
The third person is the person spoken about.
      He is late.

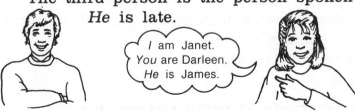

I am Janet.
You are Darleen.
He is James.

■ **Personal pronouns express number. They can be singular or plural.** Look at these examples:

Singular (one)   **Plural** (more than one)

■ **Personal pronouns express gender. The three genders are masculine** (male), **feminine** (female), **and neuter.** Look at these examples:

Masculine   **Feminine**   **Neuter**

■ **Personal pronouns express case. The case reflects the way the pronoun is used in a sentence. The three cases are nominative** (the pronoun is used as the subject), **objective** (the pronoun is used as the object), **and possessive** (the pronoun shows ownership). Look at these examples.

Nominative — *He* is in my French class.
Objective — I know *him*.
Possessive — That book is *his*.

PERSONAL PRONOUNS

	Nominative	Objective	Possessive
Singular			
First person	I	me	my, mine
Second person	you	you	your, yours
Third person	he, she, it	him, her, it	his, her, hers, its
Plural			
First person	we	us	our, ours
Second person	you	you	your, yours
Third person	they	them	their, theirs

ACTIVITY 1.   Use the chart above to help you do this activity.   Do your work like these examples:

first person, singular, nominative — *I*
second person, plural, possessive — *your, yours*
third person, singular, objective, masculine — *him*

1.   third person, plural, nominative —
2.   third person, singular, objective, neuter —
3.   first person, plural, possessive —
4.   second person, singular, objective —
5.   third person, plural, possessive —

ACTIVITY 2.   Which pronoun or pronouns could be used to replace each of the underlined words or groups of words?   Write your answers on paper.

1.   I have a hammer and a saw.
2.   The gloves are lost.
3.   An airplane is flying overhead.
4.   I wrote a letter to George.
5.   Sara's house is in the country.
6.   "That book is Janet's," Janet said.
7.   "That is Darleen and Janet's room," Janet said.
8.   "Janet is late," Darleen said.
9.   Carol and I are going to the dance.

ACTIVITY 3. On your paper, rewrite each of the sentences below. Use a pronoun to replace the noun or words which are underlined. Do yours like this example:

At the end of the first day of school, <u>Janet</u> was tired.
At the end of the first day of school, <u>she</u> was tired.

1. <u>Janet and Darleen</u> waited for the school bus.
2. "The teacher gave <u>Janet</u> homework," Janet said.
3. Janet decided to do <u>her homework</u> as soon as she got home.
4. <u>Janet's</u> homework was not difficult.
5. The teacher told <u>Janet</u> to write a paragraph in French.
6. "What is the paragraph about?" <u>Darleen</u> asked.
7. "What I did on <u>Janet's</u> vacation, of course!" Janet laughed.

ACTIVITY 4. Make a list of all the personal pronouns in these sentences. Then, next to each pronoun, write its antecedent. Do yours like this example:

Finally Darleen and Janet got on their bus.

Pronoun	Antecedent
their	*Darleen and Janet*

1. Janet had her French book.
2. She and Darleen talked all the way home.
3. They laughed about a joke they had heard.
4. "I am hungry," Janet said.
5. "You can stop by my house," Darleen said. "We can fix a hamburger."
6. "A hamburger sounds very good to me," Janet said.

You should have listed nine personal pronouns.

■ The compound personal pronouns are formed by adding -self to the singular and -selves to the plural pronouns. They are also called the "-self pronouns."

-SELF PRONOUNS		
	Singular	**Plural**
First person	myself	ourselves
Second person	yourself	yourselves
Third person	{ himself herself, itself	themselves

ACTIVITY 5. Read these sentences. Make a list of all of the -self pronouns. Write *singular* or *plural* beside each one. Do yours like the example.

Janet studied her French by herself.

herself — *singular*

1. The glass fell off the shelf by itself.
2. Darleen and Janet cleaned the kitchen themselves.
3. I myself prefer spicy food.
4. We cooked dinner by ourselves.
5. Try to answer that question by yourself.
6. Tiny sat up by himself.
7. Clean up the kitchen by yourselves.
8. She went to the movies by herself.

LESSON REVIEW. Read these sentences. Find ten personal pronouns. List them on your paper. Write the antecedent beside each one.

1. The first day of school was over. It had been very pleasant.
2. Janet enjoyed her new classes.
3. She also enjoyed seeing her old friends.
4. Janet went to her room to do her French homework by herself.
5. She wondered if James Melcher would call.
6. She hoped that he would.

LESSON TWO. RELATIVE PRONOUNS

> The relative pronouns are *who, whom, whose, which, that,* and *what.*
>
> *Who, whom,* and *whose* refer to people.
> *Which* and *what* refer to things.
> *That* refers to people or things.

ACTIVITY 1. Copy these sentences on your paper. Then circle the relative pronouns.

1. The car that Ted bought is blue and white.
2. Ted wanted a car that had four doors.
3. Ted's friend, who is a mechanic, inspected the car.
4. Ted prefers cars which have four doors.
5. Ted also had a friend whose father owned a garage.

■ **All relative pronouns have antecedents.**

ACTIVITY 2. Read these sentences. The relative pronouns are underlined. List them on your paper. Write the antecedent beside each one. Do yours like the example:

The car <u>that</u> Ted bought is blue and white.

that — *car*

1. The man <u>who</u> owned the garage sold Ted new tires.
2. There is the man <u>whom</u> I met last week.
3. Andy likes cars <u>which</u> have four-wheel drive.
4. The mechanic has a car <u>that</u> is an antique.
5. Did you see the screwdriver <u>that</u> I was using?

■ The compound relative pronouns are *whoever, whomever, whichever,* and *whatever.*

■ The antecedents of compound relative pronouns are not stated. The antecedents refer to a group of persons or things which are known to the listener or reader. Look at these examples:

ACTIVITY 3. Read these sentences. Make a list of all of the relative pronouns on your paper.

1. Do whatever you think should be done.
2. My sister, who wants to be an actress, tried out for the school play.
3. My dog, which is a poodle, barks at everyone.
4. You may have whatever you want for dinner.
5. Here are the shoes that I bought.
6. Andy had a friend whose cousin caught a forty-pound fish.
7. Whoever wants to go first should come up now.
8. I found what I wanted.

ACTIVITY 4. Read the list of words below. Find all of the pronouns and write them on your paper.

1. himself	8. bus	15. friend
2. whoever	9. lady	16. you
3. car	10. Ms. Wise	17. whatever
4. Andy	11. I	18. themselves
5. which	12. what	19. its
6. that	13. whom	20. happiness
7. he	14. school	21. she

ACTIVITY 5. Read the list of pronouns below. Make two lists on your paper. Name one list *Personal Pronouns*. Name the other list *Relative Pronouns*.

1. we	8. you	15. whom
2. that	9. who	16. whichever
3. which	10. ours	17. that
4. what	11. them	18. themselves
5. mine	12. whose	19. whoever
6. its	13. us	20. whatever
7. I	14. itself	21. he

■ **A relative pronoun must agree with its antecedent.** Remember:

> *Who, whom,* and *whose* refer to people.
> *Which* and *what* refer to things.
> *That* can refer to people or things.

ACTIVITY 6. Read each sentence. Choose the correct pronoun from the two words in parentheses. Write the complete sentence.

1. There are the shoes _____ I want. (who, that)
2. My dog, _____ is a St. Bernard, eats anything. (who, which)
3.⁺ There is the lady _____ I met last week. (whom, what)
4. I like a house _____ has a big yard. (who, that)

LESSON REVIEW. Read these sentences. Make a list of all the relative pronouns. Include the compound relative pronouns. Write the antecedent beside the pronoun. Do yours like this example:

I like food that is very spicy.

that — *food*

1. The mechanic who checked Ted's car did a good job.
2. Ted said to Andy and Frank, "Whoever wants to go for a ride should come now."
3. You may choose whichever shoes you want.
4. There is the man that I met in Florida.
5. We have steak and chicken. You may have whichever you prefer.
6. Ted had a friend whose sister was in the play.
7. Did you see the hat that I was wearing?
8. Mrs. Jones has a coat that is genuine mink.
9. I got what I wanted for my birthday.

Talk It Over

Here are some famous sayings that have relative pronouns. Discuss their meanings with your class.

He laughs best *who* laughs last.

Whoever lies on the ground cannot fall.

Whoever would find pearls must dive deep.

It is love *that* makes the world go round.

They also serve *who* only stand and wait.

LESSON THREE. PRONOUNS THAT ASK QUESTIONS

> An *interrogative pronoun* introduces a question. These pronouns are *who, which,* and *what.* Read the examples below.
>
> *Who* is planning the dance?
> *Which* shoes did Janet buy?
> *What* page is the homework assignment on?

Interrogative pronouns may also be used as relative pronouns, as you know from Lesson Two. *Who, which,* and *what* are interrogative pronouns only when they ask a question. Read these examples:

Interrogative — *Who* is going with Andy to the dance?

Relative — Andy asked a girl *who* is in his class.

The interrogative pronoun may be used to ask a question directly or indirectly. Read the examples below.

Direct Question — *What* day is the dance?

Indirect Questions — Do you know *what* day the dance is?

Tell me *what* day the dance is.

ACTIVITY 1. Read these sentences carefully. Make a list of the interrogative pronouns on your paper.

1. Which season of the year do you like best?
2. What is the name of your book?
3. Tell me who is going to the dance.
4. Do you know what the answer is?
5. Who is your favorite singer?

■ **Interrogative pronouns must agree with their antecedents. The antecedent is the answer to the question that they ask.** Read these examples:

Who refers to a person or persons.

    Who is your English teacher?

    Who are the teams in the Super Bowl this year?

What refers to things, places, or ideas.

    What is the name of your street?

    What is your answer?

Which can refer to people or things. Use **which** when the answer is a choice between two or more definite things.

    Which team will win the game?

    Which newspaper do you read?

ACTIVITY 2. Write these sentences on your paper. Choose the correct pronoun in the parentheses.

1. _____ of these fish is larger? (Which, What)
2. _____ do you want for dinner? (Which, What)
3. _____ will win the World Series? (Who, What)
4. _____ is the name of your school? (Which, What)
5. Andy wondered _____ to ask to the dance. (whom, which)
6. _____ plays third base for the team? (Who, Which)
7. _____ is the world's tallest building? (Who, What)

ACTIVITY 3. Write two sentences using each of these interrogative pronouns.

1. what
2. which
3. who

ACTIVITY 4. Read these sentences carefully. Find five relative and five interrogative pronouns. Make two lists on your paper. Do yours like the example.

Which shoes are the ones *that* you like best?

Interrogative Pronouns   **Relative Pronouns**

Question / *which*   *that*

1. Ted has a friend whose uncle lives in Canada.
2. Name all of the states that you have visited.
3. What is the name of your book?
(4.) Choose whichever book that you want.
5. Tell me which book you like best.
6. Who is the coach of your baseball team?
7. Which tree is taller?
8. What is your favorite subject in school?
9. Do whatever you think is best.

LESSON REVIEW. These sentences contain twenty pronouns. The pronouns are personal, relative, and interrogative. Find these pronouns and list them in order. Name the kind of pronoun that each one is. Do yours like this example.

Who is the man *that I* saw yesterday?

    1. Who — *interrogative*
    2. that — *relative*
    3. I — *personal*

3 1. It was Friday night. Ted and Andy wondered what they would do.
1 2. "What is playing at the movies?" Ted asked.
2 3. "Whatever is there is okay with me," Andy said.
3 4. "Whom should we ask to go with us?" Ted said.
3 5. "I think that I will ask Janet," Andy answered.
2 6. Ted thought for a moment about which girl he could ask.
6 7. "What is the name of Janet's friend? Is it Darleen? I think that I will ask her," Ted decided.

LESSON FOUR. DEMONSTRATIVE PRONOUNS

Demonstrative pronouns point out persons and things. The demonstrative pronouns are *this, these, that,* and *those.*

this and **these** – *Close*

This book is mine.   (singular)
These books are mine.   (plural)

that and **those**   *Far*

That house is expensive. (singular)
Those houses are expensive. (plural)

This and *these* point out persons and things which are close. *That* and *those* point out persons and things which are farther away.

ACTIVITY 1. Copy these sentences on your paper. Circle all of the demonstrative pronouns.

1. Did Darleen enjoy that movie?
2. Those socks are new.
3. Put these clothes in the hamper.
4. Hang that coat up, please.
5. This is my neighbor, Mrs. Loomis.
6. Those flowers are beautiful.
7. These are my favorite pictures.

ACTIVITY 2.   Read the following sentences. Choose the correct pronoun in parentheses. Write the whole sentence on your paper.

1. Did you see _____ shooting star? (this, that)
2. _____ is my house. (This, These)
3. Look across the street. _____ are new houses. (These, Those)
4. _____ people just moved in. (That, Those)
5. Mrs. Jones handed Janet a package. "You may open _____ now," she said. (this, that)

LESSON REVIEW.   You have become familiar with four kinds of pronouns. They are personal, relative, interrogative, and demonstrative. Find twenty pronouns in the sentences below. List them in order. Name the kind of pronoun that each one is. Do yours like the example.

> Who was that lady that I saw yesterday?
> 1. Who — *interrogative*
> 2. that — *demonstrative*
> 3. that — *relative*
> 4. I — *personal*

1. Ted works at a store which sells men's clothes.
2. "Which evenings am I working this week?" he asked.
3. "Whichever nights that you want." said his boss, Mr. Jackson.
4. Ted decided on the hours that he wanted.
5. "What department am I in tonight?" Ted asked.
6. "Go to the stockroom and help them with inventory."
7. Ted asked those who were working what he could do first.
8. He helped the people whose job was counting shoes.

LESSON FIVE. INDEFINITE PRONOUNS

Indefinite pronouns replace nouns that are understood by the listener or reader. These nouns may not have been mentioned in the sentence. Read this list of indefinite pronouns:

one	thing	some
someone	something	somebody
anyone	anything	anybody
everyone	everything	everybody
no one	nothing	nobody
other	none	much
another	few	all
each	several	one another
each other	many	any

ACTIVITY 1. Read these sentences. Make a list of the indefinite pronouns on your paper.

1. Everyone brought food to the picnic.
2. Jack did not know anyone at the party.
3. None of the boys was late.
4. Try to be nice to one another.
5. Few of the students liked liver.
6. Everyone talked to the bride at the wedding.
7. Every one of the people brought a present.
8. Sam saw no one that he knew.
9. Cathy knew some of the people in the class.
10. Everything is ready for the party.
11. Try to help each other.
12. Some of the food was too spicy.
13. Karl knew nothing about the Red River.
14. Sally knows someone in that neighborhood.
15. Other than Sara, I do not know a person in that school.

■ **Some indefinite pronouns are singular even though their meaning is plural.** Look at these examples.

> *Everyone* refers to one group of people.
> **Right:**   Everyone *is* going to the beach.
> **Wrong:**   Everyone *are* going to the beach.

■ **Some indefinite pronouns may be singular or plural.** You must read the sentence carefully and understand its meaning. In the examples below, the verbs show whether the pronouns are singular or plural.

Singular —"All *is* well," the town crier said.
Plural   —All of the boys *are* going to the concert.

ACTIVITY 2.   Copy these sentences. Use the correct word in the parentheses.

1. Everybody ___ coming to the party.   (is, are)
2. Everything in the closet ___ Janet's.   (is, are)
3. Some of those people ___ going home now. (is, are)
4. No one ___ a watch on.   (has, have)
5. Someone ___ reading that book.   (is, are)
6. Somebody ___ my pencil.   (has, have)

■ **The indefinite pronoun may be the antecedent for another pronoun.** Read these examples.

All of the boys ate *their* lunches.   (*All* is plural.)
Every *one* of the girls has *her* ticket.   (*One* is singular.)

■ If the gender of the indefinite pronoun is not clear, you may use the masculine pronoun. You may also use both the masculine and feminine pronouns. Look at these examples:

Each person brought *his* notebook.
Everyone bought *his* or *her* ticket.

ACTIVITY 3. Copy these sentences. Use the correct pronoun in the parentheses.

1. Everyone must leave _____ coat on. (his, their)
2. Each girl brought _____ own paper. (her, their)
3. All of the men brought _____ wives. (his, their)
4. None of the children remembered _____ lunch. (his, their)
5. Every one of those coats is missing _____ buttons. (its, their)

ACTIVITY 4. Use each of these indefinite pronouns correctly in a sentence.

1. someone
2. everyone
3. no one
4. anybody
5. nothing
6. none
7. everything
8. something
9. all
10. nobody

LESSON REVIEW. Find ten indefinite pronouns in these sentences. List them in order on your paper.

1. Everyone in Mr. Jackson's store was decorating for fall.
2. All of the employees came to work that day.
3. Everybody was quiet as he or she worked.
4. Nobody said anything.
5. Suddenly someone laughed.
6. "Why are we all so quiet?" someone said.
7. "No one had anything to say!" said Mr. Jackson.

CHAPTER REVIEW

In this chapter, you studied five kinds of pronouns. Pronouns replace nouns in sentences. You learned that a pronoun must agree with its antecedent. The antecedent is the word or words that the pronoun is replacing in a sentence.

Before you do the exercises below, review the five kinds of pronouns.

Personal Pronouns — *I, you, he, she, it, they, theirs*
Relative Pronouns — *who, which, that, whatever*
Interrogative Pronouns — *which, who, what*
Demonstrative Pronouns — *this, that, these, those*
Indefinite Pronouns — *anyone, all, nobody, everything*

Part 1. The pronouns in these sentences are underlined. Make a list of the pronouns on your paper. Beside each pronoun, write the kind of pronoun it is. Do yours like this example:

That is the one which I like best.

That — *demonstrative*	which — *relative*
one — *indefinite*	I — *personal*

1. It was the dry season of the year.
2. Everyone was watering his yard.
3. No one was expecting rain for a week.
4. "Everybody must take his or her turn," Mr. Jones announced.
5. "Who wants to water tonight?"
6. "That isn't a hard job," Janet said.
7. She went outside and watered everything thoroughly.
8. "I will take my turn tomorrow night," Ted said.
9. They did what had to be done until the rain came.

Part 2. Read each pair of sentences. Copy the correct sentence in each pair on your paper.

1. A Ted decided to build hisself a stereo.
   B Ted decided to build himself a stereo.

2. A Which kind should I buy?
   B What kind should I buy?

3. A Which of my friends will help me?
   B Who of my friends will help me?

4. A Ted chose the friend what knew the most.
   B Ted chose the friend that knew the most.

5. A Nobody are as smart about electronics as Andy.
   B Nobody is as smart about electronics as Andy.

Ted handed Andy the directions.

6. A "You can read these," he said.
   B "You can read those," he said.

7. A I think we can do this ourself.
   B I think we can do this ourselves.

8. A Us guys won't have any problem at all.
   B We guys won't have any problem at all.

9. A "I think this kit is missing some of its parts."
   B "I think this kit is missing some of it's parts."

10. A "Do whatever needs to be done," Ted said.
    B "Do whichever needs to be done," Ted said.

11. A Soon they had put the parts together theirselves.
    B Soon they had put the parts together themselves.

They looked at the finished stereo.

12. A The music this will play will be terrific!
    B The music that will play will be terrific!

3

Adjectives—Words That Describe Nouns and Pronouns

> An adjective is a word that describes a noun or pronoun. Adjectives may be used to limit or change the meaning of a noun or pronoun.

■ **Most adjectives come before the noun they are describing.**

The sleepy **child** was crying.

■ **Adjectives which describe pronouns come later in the sentence.**

He is *tired* and *hungry*.

■ **Adjectives are sometimes placed after the noun for emphasis. They are set off from the rest of the sentence with commas.**

The **tree**, *wet* and *shimmering*, swayed in the breeze.

WARM-UP 1. Find eleven adjectives in these sentences. List them on your paper in order.

1. The autumn day was cool and clear.

2. Everyone was happy about the beautiful weather.

3. After school, Janet and Darleen went for a long walk.

4. They admired nature, wondrous and splendid.

■ **Every adjective in a sentence describes a noun or pronoun in that sentence.**

WARM-UP 2. List the underlined adjectives on your paper. Next to each, write the noun or pronoun being described. Do yours like this example:

The new car was expensive.
The — car
new — car
expensive — car

1. The students in Janet's homeroom had a meeting.
2. They elected new officers for the school year.
3. "Janet is smart, loyal, and fun," said Darleen.
4. "She will be a good president."
5. The election was close, but Janet won.

■ **Nouns and pronouns can sometimes be used as adjectives.**

WARM-UP 3. List the underlined words in these sentences on your paper. Next to each, identify the part of speech. It will be a noun or adjective.

1. That history book belongs to James Melcher.
2. James takes history during the second period.
3. They all went to the meeting room.
4. The meeting began at three o'clock.
5. The south wind was warm.
6. The wind came from the south.

List these underlined words. Write *pronoun* or *adjective* next to each.

7. That is my homeroom.
8. That room is mine.
9. The tree had lost almost all its leaves.
10. Her brother called her.

Now, you are ready to begin the first lesson.

LESSON ONE. WHAT IS AN ADJECTIVE?

> An adjective is a word that describes a noun or pronoun. An adjective can name a characteristic of someone or something.
>
> The *sleepy* child is crying.
> She is *sleepy.*
> That is a *wonderful* idea.
>
> An adjective can limit the noun by giving a number or quantity.
>
> There are *three* trees.
> *Several* people arrived late.

■ **The demonstrative pronouns can be used as adjectives.**

Did you see *that* boy?
Those people are in my class.

■ **The articles "a," "an," and "the" are always used as adjectives.**

I saw *the* movie yesterday.
Janet ate *an* apple for lunch.
Andy caught *a* fish.

■ **Possessive nouns and pronouns can be used as adjectives.**

Darleen went to *her* class.
Ted and Andy saw *their* favorite movie.
Andy's house is on the corner.

ACTIVITY 1. List the adjectives in these sentences.

3 1. Ted has a part-time job at Mr. Jackson's store.
3 2. The store sells sporting goods and men's clothes.
2 3. Ted works in many different departments.
2 4. His favorite department is fishing equipment.
3 5. "Those new reels are expensive," Ted thought.
1 6. "I will save my money and buy one."

■ **The adjective always describes a noun or pronoun within the sentence.**

Ted was *late* for work. (*Late* describes *Ted*.)

Ted sells *men's* clothes. (*Men's* describes *clothes*.)

The store opened at noon. (*The* describes *store*.)

ACTIVITY 2. Read these sentences. All of the adjectives are underlined. List them on your paper. Beside each adjective, write the noun or pronoun that is described. Do yours like these examples:

> She is <u>tall</u>.   <u>The</u> <u>old</u> house is for sale.
>
> tall — she   The — house
>   old — house

1. Ted bought <u>an</u> <u>expensive</u> <u>new</u> reel.
2. He planned <u>a</u> <u>fishing</u> trip with <u>his</u> friend.
3. "<u>This</u> reel will be <u>great</u>," he said.
4. "I am <u>sure</u> that I will catch <u>several</u> <u>big</u> fish."
5. Ted and Andy left early <u>the</u> <u>next</u> morning.
6. They were very <u>hopeful</u>.

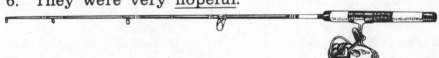

ACTIVITY 3. Read these sentences. Find the adjectives. List them on your paper. Beside each adjective, write the noun or pronoun that is described.

1. The lake was beautiful on that morning.
2. Ted saw a large fish jump in the water.
3. Andy used his trusty old rod and reel.
4. They fished for eight hours.
5. By late afternoon they had caught many fish.
6. They were tired and happy with themselves.

■ **Adjectives help make your meaning clear. They can make a sentence more interesting, too.**

Jake was ready for dinner.

Tall, mean Jake was ready for *a big* dinner.

ACTIVITY 4. Rewrite these sentences on your paper. Add one or more adjectives before each noun. The nouns are underlined.

1. <u>Students</u> brought <u>books</u> to <u>class</u>.
2. <u>People</u> brought <u>food</u>.
3. <u>School</u> started early.
4. I saw <u>mountains</u> and <u>rivers</u>.
5. Darleen planted <u>tomatoes</u> and <u>cucumbers</u>.

ACTIVITY 5. Write five sentences about the picture below on your paper. Use as many adjectives as you can. Circle all of the adjectives in your sentences.

■ **Adjectives can tell several things about a person or thing in a sentence.**

I live in *that large white colonial* house.

Which one?	*that* one
How big?	*large*
What color?	*white*
What kind?	*colonial*

ACTIVITY 6. Add as many adjectives as you can to these sentences. Write the new sentences on your paper. Circle all of the adjectives in your sentences.

1. Darleen has a dog.
2. Ted bought a coat for his sister.
3. The fisherman cast his line into the lake.
4. It was morning.
5. The store had a sale.

LESSON REVIEW. Find ten adjectives in these sentences. Make a list of the adjectives on your paper. Beside each one, write the noun or pronoun that the adjective describes in the sentence.

1. In October the weather can be chilly.
2. Ted decided to wear his winter coat.
3. He had several classes on Wednesdays.
4. Ted's favorite class was math.
5. Math was easy for him.
6. He drove to the college in his car.

LESSON TWO. THE ARTICLES—*A, AN, THE*

> The articles, "a," "an," and "the," are **adjectives.** They are placed before nouns in sentences.

■ **The definite article is "the."** Use *the* when you are talking about a particular person or thing.

■ **The indefinite articles are "a" and "an."** Use *a* or *an* when you are talking about a general group of people or things.

Give me <u>the</u> book.   Give me <u>a</u> book.
(A certain book.)   *(Any book will do.)*

ACTIVITY 1. Copy these sentences on your paper. Circle all of the articles.

1. The math class was the first class of the day.
2. The students had a homework assignment.
3. The first part of the class was easy.
4. The class discussed the answers to the problems.
5. "I got a different answer to the problem," Ted said.
6. The teacher explained the problem.
7. She used an overhead projector.
8. Later she made a new assignment.
9. The class was an hour long.

■ Use the article "a" before a word that begins with a consonant sound. Use the article "an" before a word that begins with a vowel sound.

a large apple   a tough assignment
an apple   an assignment

ACTIVITY 2. Copy these sentences on your paper. Use the correct article in the parentheses after each.

1. Darleen packed ____ apple for her lunch. (a, an)
2. They waited for ____ hour. (a, an)
3. The teacher made ____ long assignment. (a, an)
4. They had ____ English lesson. (a, an)
5. The children fed ____ elephant at the zoo. (a, an)
6. We built ____ igloo in our backyard. (a, an)
7. Look up the topic in ____ index. (a, an)
8. The principal posted ____ honor roll. (a, an)
9. Not ____ one of them was late. (a, an)
10. Jack is ____ honest man. (a, an)

■ The article "a" is used with singular nouns. The article "the" can be used with singular and plural nouns.

I bought a car. (*Car* is singular.)
Ted bought the car. (*Car* is singular.)
He bought the books. (*Books* is plural.)

ACTIVITY 3. Copy these sentences on your paper. Choose the correct article in the parentheses for each.

1. Look at ____ coat with the fur collar. (a, the)
2. Did you enjoy eating ____ peaches? (a, the)
3. Mrs. Jones put ____ groceries on the table. (a, the)
4. We went to New York City to see ____ play. (an, the)
5. Chicago is ____ American city. (a, an)
6. They did ____ activity in class. (a, the)

LESSON REVIEW. Number your paper from 1 to 10. Write the correct article for each sentence.

1. A hammer is _____ useful tool. (a, an)
2. Did you see _____ pencils I left here? (a, the)
3. Where is _____ envelope? (a, an)
4. I was in _____ earthquake in California. (a, an)
5. We have _____ eight-foot tree in our yard. (a, an)
6. Have you ever seen _____ bald eagle? (a, an)
7. At the zoo we looked at _____ snakes. (a, the)
8. They did _____ math activity. (a, an)
9. "What _____ ugly dog," she said. (a, an)
10. What happened to _____ umbrella? (a, the)

ADJECTIVES ARE WORDS OF POWER

We can say so much with just one word if it is the RIGHT word. Read the sentences below. Select the meaning of each italicized word.

1. The oceans of the world are so deep that they seem *abysmal.*
   a. bottomless   b. beautiful   c. frightening
2. Darleen is really *meticulous;* she works slowly so she won't make even one mistake.
   a. sloppy   b. brilliant   c. unusually careful
3. "I will not change my decision," said the man. "It is *irrevocable.*"
   a. logical   b. changeable   c. unchangeable
4. Sam and Fred shouted and punched each other in the middle of a *virulent* argument.
   a. loud   b. hostile and bitter   c. silly

LESSON THREE: ADJECTIVES THAT ARE CAPITALIZED

> Proper adjectives are proper nouns used as adjectives or adjective forms of proper nouns.
>
> **Proper noun** — He is an *American*.
> **Proper adjective** — He is an *American* soldier.
>
> **Proper noun** — I went to visit *France*.
> **Proper adjective** — I enjoyed the *French* food.

ACTIVITY 1. Read these sentences. Make a list of the proper adjectives on your paper. Not all of the capitalized words will be proper adjectives, so read very carefully.

1. Janet had French first period.
2. She almost forgot her French book.
3. In her English class, Janet was studying Shakespearean literature.
4. She liked American literature better.
5. Mr. Thomas was teaching them about Indians in social studies.
6. He brought in some Indian blankets and jewelry to show the class.
7. Then Janet went to her career education class. It was a Wednesday-only class.

ACTIVITY 2. Use these proper adjectives in a sentence. Be sure that you use them as adjectives that describe nouns or pronouns.

1. Spanish
2. German
3. Chinese
4. Democratic
5. French
6. Swiss
7. American
8. Olympic

ACTIVITY 3. Copy these sentences on your paper. Add a proper adjective in each space.

1. We ordered _____ dressing.
2. Mr. Jones likes _____ cheese.
3. Darleen studied the _____ language last year.
4. Those people are _____ citizens.
5. He belongs to the _____ political party.
6. The class studied _____ tribes of Mexico.
7. Harry Smith is a _____ artist.
8. He just bought a _____ truck.

ACTIVITY 4. Each of these sentences has an underlined word. Decide if the word is a noun or an adjective. Number your paper from 1 to 10. Write your answer beside each number.

1. I like French designers.
2. Mark lives in Philadelphia.
3. He is a Philadelphia boy.
4. Frank is as normal as blueberry pie.
5. He wore an Irish derby on St. Patrick's Day.
6. I am late for my French lesson.
7. Next summer I want to visit Spain.
8. I'd like to study Spanish first.
9. Where is my Spanish book?
10. The book is in the Chevrolet truck.

LESSON REVIEW. Copy these sentences on your paper. Capitalize all of the proper adjectives.

1. Darleen has a french poodle named Tiny.
2. Tiny likes to ride in the ford truck.
3. Tiny also likes swiss cheese.
4. The rest of the family prefers american cheese.
5. That poodle thinks he is a swiss dog.
6. Tiny is actually quite famous. A spanish artist painted him.

LESSON FOUR. POSSESSIVES USED AS ADJECTIVES

Some adjectives are really nouns or pronouns in the possessive case. In a sentence these words are used to describe. They are used as adjectives.

Possessive nouns used as adjectives:
> *Darleen's* dog is a poodle.
> We went to the *world's* fair.
> There is *Mr. Jackson's* store.

Possessive pronouns used as adjectives:
> *My* house is on the corner.
> That wagon has lost *its* wheels.
> *Whose* room is that?

The possessive noun or pronoun tells us something about the noun it is describing.

ACTIVITY 1. In these sentences the possessives used as adjectives are underlined. Make a list of them on your paper. Beside each one, write the noun that the word is describing. Do yours like this example:

His cap was left in Mr. Jackson's store.

His — cap

Mr. Jackson's — store

1. I always like to get my money's worth.
2. Naturally I shop in Mr. Jackson's store.
3. His store is close to my house.
4. In the men's department there were some wool sweaters.
5. I bought one for my father's birthday.
6. His birthday will be next Saturday.
7. I still remember our fun buying last year's presents.
8. Dad's face lit up when he opened them.

■ **A possessive noun can be described by a possessive adjective.**

That is _my_ _sister's_ book.

_My_ describes _sister's_. Whose sister?

Sister's describes _book._ Whose book?

ACTIVITY 2. Find the possessives used as adjectives. List them on your paper. Also write the noun the adjective is describing.

1. Jack's bike is missing.
2. His coat was in the living room.
3. My mother's ring was lost.
4. There was a rabbit in my garden.
5. Whose pencil is this?

LESSON REVIEW. Find eleven possessives used as adjectives in these sentences. List them on your paper in order. Beside each one, write the noun that the adjective is describing.

1. Ted and Andy did their math homework together.
2. Andy's answer to problem 7 was wrong.
3. "Explain your answer to me," Andy said.
4. Ted tried to explain his answer.
5. There was a frown on Andy's face.
6. "Maybe my answer is wrong, too," Ted said.
7. "Let's both check our work," Andy suggested.
8. Andy's suggestion was helpful.
9. "Now, let's get some of your mother's great dessert," Andy said.
10. Together they raided Ted's refrigerator.

LESSON FIVE. NUMBERS USED AS ADJECTIVES

> Numbers can be used as adjectives. The number describes the noun by telling *how many*.
>
> Mrs. Jones canned *twenty* jars of pears.
> *Seventeen* people came to the party.
>
> The indefinite pronoun can also be used as an adjective. The indefinite pronoun suggests a number. The exact amount is not given.
>
> *Several* years went by before I saw her.
> They lived in that house *many* years.
> *All* students must report to class.

ACTIVITY 1. Here is a list of ten words which can be used as adjectives. Use each one in a sentence. Be sure you are using the word as an adjective which describes a noun or pronoun.

1. few
2. eighty
3. one
4. some
5. three

6. much
7. most
8. thirty-three
9. several
10. all

ACTIVITY 2. Read these sentences. The underlined words are adjectives. List them on your paper. Write the noun that each word describes beside it. Do yours like this example:

<u>Many</u> people read that book.   Many — people

1. <u>Twenty-five</u> people signed up for the class.
2. <u>One</u> student dropped out.
3. After a <u>few</u> weeks the teacher gave a test.
4. <u>Several</u> members of the class got 100 percent.
5. <u>Most</u> students enjoyed the class.

ACTIVITY 3. Read these sentences. All of the adjectives that number are underlined. List them on your paper. Identify which part of speech each one is. Do yours like this example.

All of the students signed up for six classes.

All — pronoun

six — adjective

1. The hurricane winds were eighty miles an hour.
2. The storm lasted for several hours.
3. Everyone on the block watched the storm.
4. Many trees blew down in the neighborhood.
5. We watched as a few cars drove through the storm.
6. Most people stayed inside.
7. The electricity was out for six hours.
8. No one could cook dinner or watch television.
9. Some families went out for dinner.
10. Others tried to barbecue in their yards.
11. The storm was the topic of conversation for many weeks.

LESSON REVIEW. List ten adjectives in these sentences. Beside each, write the noun it describes.

1. On Sunday, several friends visited City Zoo.
2. They fed peanuts to three chimpanzees.
3. Sara counted eight lions and six tigers.
4. There were many monkeys.
5. William ate three hot dogs and drank some lemonade.
6. "All birds seem to like to sing," Joyce said.
7. "I would like to stay here several hours."
8. Few people wanted to go home.

LESSON SIX. DEMONSTRATIVE ADJECTIVES

The demonstrative pronouns — this, that, these, and those — can be used as adjectives. They answer the question, "Which one?"

Remember, a word is an adjective when it describes a noun or pronoun.

<u>That</u> is a mistake. (pronoun)

<u>That</u> mistake was Andy's. (adjective)

ACTIVITY 1. In these sentences the demonstratives are underlined. Decide which ones are used as adjectives and which ones are used as pronouns.

1. "<u>This</u> Sunday let's get together and watch the football game," Andy said.
2. "Do you think <u>that</u> team will win a game <u>this</u> year?" Ted asked.
3. "Some of <u>those</u> new players are better," Andy answered.
4. "I especially like <u>that</u> new fullback from Penn State."
5. "<u>This</u> should be a good season," Ted said.
6. "<u>That</u> remains to be seen," said Andy.

LESSON REVIEW. Copy these sentences. Circle five demonstrative adjectives. Then draw an arrow to the noun each describes, like this:

Those players are on our team.

1. The football game that day was exciting.
2. "Where are those snacks you promised?"
3. "Look in that cupboard over the refrigerator."
4. "That is where my mother keeps those things."
5. "These potato chips look good. Now where are the sodas?"

LESSON SEVEN. USING ADJECTIVES TO MAKE COMPARISONS

Many adjectives are used to compare people or things. There are three degrees of comparison. The three degrees are *positive, comparative,* and *superlative.*

Positive	Comparative	Superlative
strong	stronger	strongest
easy	easier	easiest
big	bigger	biggest
careful	more careful	most careful
popular	less popular	least popular
good	better	best
bad	worse	worst

■ **Use the comparative degree to compare two things.**

■ **Use the superlative degree to compare more than two things.**

> **Right:** Sam is *younger* than Roger.
> **Wrong:** Ted is Janet's brother. He is the *oldest.*
>
> (If there are only two people, use the comparative degree.)

■ **Most one-syllable adjectives form their comparative and superlative degrees by adding -er and -est.**

ACTIVITY 1. List these adjectives on your paper. Write the comparative and superlative degrees beside each one. Do yours like this example.

tall — taller, tallest

1. young
2. old
3. kind
4. short
5. green
6. slow
7. late
8. strict
9. bright
10. nice

■ Some two-syllable adjectives form their comparative and superlative degrees by adding -er and -est. Others form their comparative and superlative degrees by using "more" and "most."

Positive	Comparative	Superlative
careful	more careful	most careful
happy	happier	happiest

■ Compare adjectives of more than two syllables by using "more" and "most" or "less" and "least."

Positive	Comparative	Superlative
wonderful	more wonderful	most wonderful
successful	more successful	most successful
excited	less excited	least excited
generous	less generous	least generous

ACTIVITY 2. Read these sentences. The adjectives are underlined. List them on your paper. Beside each one, identify the degree of comparison. Do yours like the examples.

> Fred is the <u>most helpful</u> person I know.
> That blanket is <u>soft</u>.
> She is <u>stronger</u> than her sister.

>> most helpful — superlative
>> soft — positive
>> stronger — comparative

1. That is the <u>least comfortable</u> chair.
2. Joyce thought the movie was <u>terrible</u>.
3. The girl was the <u>most talented</u> actress in the play.
4. I have never seen a <u>sadder</u> face.
5. This coat is <u>less expensive</u> than the other one.

More, most, less, and *least* are adverbs of degree. You will learn about adverbs in Chapter 6.

ACTIVITY 3. List these adjectives on your paper. Write the comparative and superlative degrees beside each one.

1.	small	6.	soft
2.	useful	7.	comfortable
3.	fast	8.	smart
4.	famous	9.	vicious
5.	stern	10.	horrible

■ **Some adjectives form their comparative and superlative degrees in an irregular way.**

Positive	Comparative	Superlative
good	better	best
bad	worse	worst

ACTIVITY 4. Use each of the following adjectives correctly in a sentence.

1.	least useful	6.	better
2.	smaller	7.	worst
3.	most successful	8.	heaviest
4.	more wonderful	9.	lighter
5.	less careful	10.	best

ACTIVITY 5. Put these fourteen adjectives into three groups. Title the groups: *Positive, Comparative, Superlative.*

1.	bad	8.	less comfortable
2.	prettier	9.	most generous
3.	less beautiful	10.	least horrible
4.	worse	11.	worst
5.	more careful	12.	popular
6.	easiest	13.	good
7.	young	14.	thinnest

ACTIVITY 6. Read each pair of sentences. Write the correct sentence on your paper.

A 1. That is the reddest sunset I have ever seen.
   That is the most red sunset I have ever seen.

B 2. Which of those two buildings is taller?
   Which of those two buildings is tallest?

A 3. Janet hopes to be thinner in two weeks.
   Janet hopes to be more thin in two weeks.

B 4. St. Augustine is the oldest city in Florida.
   St. Augustine is the older city in Florida.

A 5. This chair is the more comfortable of the two.
   This chair is the most comfortable of the two.

B 6. That movie was the goodest I have seen.
   That movie was the best I have seen.

A 7. Yesterday's homework was easier than today's.
   Yesterday's homework was easiest than today's.

B 8. Roger is the least generous person I know.
   Roger is the less generous person I know.

A 9. Karen is successfuller than Mac.
   Karen is more successful than Mac.

LESSON REVIEW. List the ten underlined adjectives. Identify the degree of comparison of each adjective.

1. Ted is <u>older</u> than Janet.
2. He is usually <u>nice</u> to Janet, but Janet thinks that Andy is <u>nicer</u>.
3. They both think that tennis is <u>fun</u>.
4. Janet's forehand was <u>better</u> than her backhand.
5. "My serve is my <u>best</u> shot," Ted said.
6. Of the two of them, Ted was the <u>better</u> player.
7. Although Janet was <u>strong</u>, Ted was <u>stronger</u>.
8. Janet decided that it was <u>easier</u> to play tennis with Darleen.

CHAPTER REVIEW

In Chapter 3 you found adjectives in sentences and used them correctly. Remember that a word is an adjective only if it describes a noun or pronoun in a sentence.

Read these sentences. Find all of the adjectives. List them in order on your paper. Beside each adjective, write the noun or pronoun that it describes. Do yours like this example:

The autumn day was cool and clear.

The — *day*

autumn — *day*

cool — *day*

clear — *day*

1. Ted and Andy decided to have a Halloween party.
2. The party was on a Saturday evening.
3. Ted's parents gave their permission.
4. They decorated the living room with orange and black streamers.
5. They bought the most horrible skeletons and the ugliest witches in the store.
6. Janet found some old decorations in the attic.
7. They bought fifty red apples and ten gallons of cider.
8. Andy carved an enormous pumpkin.
9. Several people brought more food.
10. Later everyone agreed that the party was the best one yet.

4

The Action Verb

A verb is a word in a sentence that expresses action or a state of being.

Look at these examples:

Action Verb — The Wilson Wildcats *played* their first game on Saturday.

The verb *played* expresses action. What did the Wilson Wildcats do? They *played* a game.

State-of-Being Verb — The team *looked* good.

The verb *looked* expresses a state of being. The sentence does not tell you what the team did. The sentence tells you about the team's state of being. They *looked* good.

Action Verb — Janet *looked* for Darleen.

The verb *looked* expresses action. Janet did something. She *looked* for Darleen.

In Chapter 4, you will study the action verb. Then, in Chapter 5, you will study the verbs which express a state of being.

In Chapter 4, you will:

1. Locate action verbs in sentences.
2. Use action verbs correctly.

Before you begin the lessons in Chapter 4, do the Chapter Warm-Ups. They will help you and your teacher find out how much you already know about locating verbs and using them correctly.

WARM-UP 1. Read these sentences. Find the verb in each sentence. Copy it on your paper. Do yours like the example:

Ted read the newspaper every morning.

read

1. The paper carrier brought the newspaper at six o'clock every day.
2. Mr. Jones heard a thud at the front door.
3. He opened the door.
4. Then he got his paper.
5. He carried it into the house.
6. Mr. Jones poured himself a cup of coffee.
7. He sat at the kitchen table.
8. First he read the front page.
9. Next he turned to the sports page.
10. Mr. Jones started every day the same way.

■ **A verb phrase contains a main verb and a helping verb.**

Mr. Jones *has poured* his coffee.

main verb — *poured*

helping verb — *has*

Now he *must go* to work.

main verb — *go*

helping verb — *must*

WARM-UP 2. Read these sentences. Find the verb phrase in each one. List the verb phrases on your paper.

1. By six-thirty Mr. Jones has left for work.

2. Soon he is driving down Route 50.

3. All of the traffic is rushing down the highway.

4. Most of the people are going to work.

5. Everyone is thinking about the day ahead.

WARM-UP 3. Choose the correct form of the verb to use in each sentence. Write your answers on your paper.

1. Mr. Jones has _____ to work. (went, gone)

2. He _____ down Route 50 every day. (drive, drives)

3. Sometimes he must _____ for gas. (stop, stopped)

4. At seven o'clock he _____ at his job. (arrive, arrives)

5. Mr. Jones _____ for the United States Postal Service. (work, works)

Now, you are ready to begin Lesson One.

LESSON ONE. FINDING THE VERB IN A SENTENCE

A verb is a word that expresses the action in a sentence. The verb tells what someone or something does, did, or will do.

Mr. Jones _read_ the newspaper.

Then he _went_ to work.

He _drove_ his car on Route 50.

He _arrived_ at seven o'clock.

The subject of a sentence is usually the person or thing that is doing something. The subject is the person or thing that is being talked about. The subject is a noun or pronoun.

Read the sentences below. Each subject is underlined.

The _traffic_ is rushing down the highway.

The _people_ are going to work.

Mr. Jones works for the Postal Service.

Find the verb in a sentence by asking yourself two questions:

1. Who or what is doing something? (subject)
2. What are they doing? (verb)

ACTIVITY 1. Read these sentences. Find the verbs. List them on your paper.

1. Mr. Jones parked his car.
2. He greeted several of his friends.
3. They walked into the building together.
4. Mr. Jones went to his desk.
5. Then he started his work for the day.

■ **An action verb tells what the subject does.**

ACTIVITY 2. List the subjects and verbs in these sentences. Do yours like this example:

The secretary answered the telephone.

Subject	**Verb**
secretary	*answered*

1. In the office everyone worked hard.
2. Some people sorted mail.
3. Others loaded the mail on trucks.
4. The trucks hauled the mail to other places.
5. Mail carriers deliver mail.
6. The mail goes to homes and offices.
7. Mr. Jones works in an office.
8. He prepares the payroll.
9. He gives information to the computers.
10. The computer prints the checks.

■ **A sentence can have more than one verb.**

ACTIVITY 3. Find the verb or verbs in each sentence. List them as you see in this example:

The workers went to their desks and worked.

went, worked

1. Mr. Jones parked his car and entered the building.
2. He drank some coffee and ate a doughnut.
3. He read a note from his boss.
4. His boss scheduled a meeting at ten o'clock.
5. The telephone rang.
6. Mr. Jones picked up the phone and said, "Hello."
7. He talked to the person and then hung up.
8. Then he returned to his work.
9. Another employee walked by his desk.
10. Mr. Jones looked up and smiled.

■ **Some verbs express action that cannot be seen.**

Mr. Jones _likes_ his work.

He _thinks_ about his ten o'clock meeting.

ACTIVITY 4. Find the subject in each sentence. Then find the verb. List the verbs on your paper.

1. Mr. Jones had a meeting with his boss.
2. Later he thought about the meeting.
3. The boss had a problem.
4. Mr. Jones wondered about the solution.
5. Finally he decided on the answer.
6. He knew the answer to the problem.

ACTIVITY 5. Use each verb below in a sentence. Underline each subject once and each verb twice.

1. accept
2. balance
3. comfort
4. contain
5. examine
6. have
7. lift
8. pronounce
9. remember
10. wander

LESSON REVIEW. List the verbs in these sentences.

1. Many different people work at the post office.
2. Letters and packages stream into the post office all day and night.
3. Mail carriers collect mail from mailboxes.
4. Mail comes to the post office on trucks.
5. Airplanes also bring mail in.
6. At the post office, mail handlers unload mail.
7. Postal clerks then sort the mail.
8. People put some mail on different trucks.
9. Carriers deliver local mail the next day.
10. Every post office processes huge amounts of mail every day.

LESSON TWO. VERBS ALSO EXPRESS TENSE

> The verb in a sentence also expresses *tense*. Tense means time.
>
> Verbs use endings, helping verbs, or both to express tense.
>
> The verb form without endings is called the infinitive form. The infinitive form is the same as the present tense in most cases. The past tense of regular verbs is formed by adding *-ed* to the infinitive. To express future tense, use the helping verb *will* or *shall* with the infinitive.
>
> **Infinitive**   — (to) *fish*
>
> **Present Tense** — I *fish* in that lake.
>
> **Past Tense**   — I *fished* in that lake.
>
> **Future Tense** — I *will* *fish* in that lake.

ACTIVITY 1. Read each of these sentences. The verb is underlined. Identify the tense of the verb in each sentence. Write your answers on your paper.

1. The Wilson Wildcats <u>will play</u> their first football game on Saturday.
2. The team <u>practices</u> every day.
3. They <u>wondered</u> about their opponents.
4. The coach <u>called</u> the team together.
5. He <u>talked</u> to them about the game plan.
6. "I <u>believe</u> in you guys."
7. The team <u>knows</u> the plan.
8. They <u>want</u> a victory on Saturday.

■ **Add -s to the present tense of the verb if the subject is singular.**

Singular subject—James _practices_ every day.
Plural subject — The players _practice_ every day.

Remember: Nouns which are names of groups are singular. Indefinite pronouns, such as _everyone_, are also singular.

Singular subject—The team _practices_ after school.
Plural subject — Both teams _practice_ after school.
Singular subject—Everyone _wants_ a victory.

ACTIVITY 2.   Choose the correct verb form to use in each sentence below.   Write it on your paper.

1. James _____ for a victory. (hope, hopes)
2. He _____ tackle on the team. (play, plays)
3. He _____ to practice every day. (go, goes)
4. George and Harry both _____ quarterback. (play, plays)
5. The coach _____ which one will start. (decide, decides)
6. Everyone _____ forward to the games. (look, looks)
7. The whole team _____ hard. (work, works)

The Perfect Tenses

■ **The three simple tenses are:** present, past, and future.

■ **The three perfect tenses are:** present perfect, past perfect, and future perfect.

Present Perfect — James *has tackled* his opponent.

Past Perfect — James *had tackled* him before.

Future Perfect — In a few minutes, our team *will have won* the game.

The perfect tenses are also called the *compound tenses*. The perfect tense is formed by combining the helping verb *have* with the past form of the verb. Most verbs in the English language are regular. A regular verb forms the past tense by adding -*ed*. *Have* is an irregular verb. You must learn the different forms of *have* so that you can write the perfect tenses correctly.

(To) Have

Present Tense (sing.)	— James *has* the football.
(plural)	— They *have* nine points
Past Tense	— The team *had* the lead.
Future Tense	— The team *will have* a victory.
Present Perfect (sing.)	— He *has had* an injury.
(plural)	— They *have had* the ball.
Past Perfect	— They *had had* enough.
Future Perfect	— We *will have had* a winning season.

ACTIVITY 3. Copy these sentences on your paper. Choose the correct form of the verb *have* for each.

1. The Wilson Wildcats _____ the football. (has, have)
2. The team _____ scored a touchdown. (has, have)
3. The Wildcats have _____ the ball for most of the quarter. (have, had)
4. The other team will _____ had few chances. (has, have)
5. We soon will _____ the victory. (have, had)

■ **The verb "have" can be a main verb or a helping verb.**

"Have" as a main verb—I *have* a good team.

"Have" as a
> **helping verb** —I *have scored* a touchdown.

ACTIVITY 4. Decide whether *have* is the main verb or the helping verb in each sentence. Do your work on your own paper.

1. The quarterback *has* had a good day.
2. He *has* thrown several good passes.
3. Howard *has* a good record so far.
4. He *has* one win and no losses.
5. He *has* high hopes for the future.

ACTIVITY 5. Write the present perfect, past perfect, and future perfect tenses in sentences for each verb below. Do yours like this example:

jump — He *has jumped*. He *had jumped*. He *will have jumped*.

1. act
2. discuss
3. improve
4. lock
5. move

6. offer
7. open
8. pass
9. snarl
10. whisper

■ **When a verb ends in -y and the letter before the -y is a consonant, change the -y to -i and then add the ending.**

> I *worry* every day.
> She never *worries*.
> He *worried* all day.

ACTIVITY 6. Use a form of the verb in the parentheses to complete each sentence. List the verbs. Spell them correctly on your paper.

1. Yesterday Darleen _____ tennis. (play)
2. Andy _____ for a job last week. (apply)
3. Janet _____ a new dress once a month. (buy)
4. Last year James _____ on the football team. (play)
5. Ted _____ last week's football game. (enjoy)
6. This morning they _____ to school. (hurry)
7. Sandra _____ to Aunt Emily's letter. (reply)
8. Yesterday he _____ home from school. (stay)
9. A loud thunderstorm _____ me. (terrify)
10. The witness _____ for two days during the trial. (testify)

ACTIVITY 7. Write all six tenses of each verb below, using the third person singular (he, she, or it). Do yours like this example:

whisper
present — She *whispers.*
past — She *whispered.*
future — She *will whisper.*
present perfect — She *has whispered.*
past perfect — She *had whispered.*
future perfect — She *will have whispered.*

1. walk   2. work   3. fish   4. drive   5. roar

Remember: Most verbs in the English language are regular. They form their past and perfect tenses by adding *-ed* to their present form.

■ **An irregular verb is one that does not form its past tense and perfect tense by adding -ed.**

■ **The past participle is used with "have," "has," or "had" to form the perfect tense of irregular verbs.** Look at these commonly-used irregular verbs.

Present	Past	had, has, or Past Participle
begin	began	(have) begun
catch	caught	(have) caught
choose	chose	(have) chosen
come	came	(have) come
eat	ate	(have) eaten
give	gave	(have) given
go	went	(have) gone
know	knew	(have) known
see	saw	(have) seen
teach	taught	(have) taught

ACTIVITY 8. Copy these sentences. Use the correct form of each verb in parentheses.

1. Ms. Lee has _____ math for many years. (teach)
2. Carol _____ her old bike to her sister. (give)
3. Howard _____ an old friend at the movies. (see)
4. They have already _____ their dinner. (eat)
5. Have you ever _____ that movie? (see)
6. Fred had _____ his homework already. (begin)
7. Jackie _____ the answer to the question. (know)
8. The fielder _____ the deep fly ball. (catch)
9. The news _____ on TV at six o'clock. (come)
10. Where has Mildred _____ ? (go)
11. Saturday everyone _____ to the game. (go)
12. I finally have _____ my new coat. (choose)

■ The words in a verb phrase may be together, or they may be separated by another word in the sentence.

> Has Donna gone to the store?
> She has finally written the letter.
> Michael will probably do his work.

ACTIVITY 9. List the verb phrases in these sentences on your paper.

1. James has always given his best.
2. That bell has never rung on time.
3. Have you heard that record before?
4. Victor has often seen him before.
5. I have not seen him before.
6. Have you ever studied French?
7. Carl will probably bring his lunch.
8. Jane and Sam have never gone to a museum.
9. She had always had good luck.
10. Barbara had seldom enjoyed a book so much.

ACTIVITY 10. Write the tense of each verb or verb phrase which is underlined.

1. Will you drive me to the store?
2. Yesterday Beth lost her gloves.
3. Ms. Potter teaches my math class.
4. The coach finally chose all of the players.
5. The Wildcats will play on Saturday.
6. Most of the students came to the game.
7. Janet had known most of the players for years.
8. A reporter has written about the game.
9. The story will appear in tomorrow's paper.
10. By noon everyone in town will have read it.

LESSON REVIEW. Read the story below. Find all the verbs or verb phrases. List them on your paper. Write the tense beside each one.

Wildcats Devour Lincoln Lions

On Saturday, September 30, the Wilson Wildcat fans enjoyed a 21-3 victory over the Lincoln Lions.

Quarterback George Benetez threw two touchdown passes in the first half. The half ended at 14-0.

James Melcher made a big play late in the final quarter. He had tackled the Lions' running back. He fumbled the ball. The Wildcats recovered on their 48-yard line. Wilson marched down the field and scored the final goal.

Many fans will have already extended congratulations to Melcher. We offer ours now for a fine play.

The Lions' only score came in the third quarter with a field goal.

Next week the Wildcats will face the Crofton Cougars. The team hopes for a winning season. They have looked forward to the county championship for many years.

LESSON THREE. THE PROGRESSIVE FORMS

The progressive forms of verbs express continuing action. Compare the two sentences below.

Janet *practices* the trumpet. (present)
Janet *is practicing* the trumpet.
(present progressive)
A progressive form is a verb phrase.
"Be" + the present participle

The present tense of the verb with the ending "-ing" is called the present participle.
Read the examples below. The verb is "work."

Present progressive - He *is working.*
Past progressive - He *was working.*
Future progressive - He *will be working.*
Present perfect progressive - He *has been working.*
Past perfect progressive - He *had been working.*
Future perfect progressive - He *will have been working.*

ACTIVITY 1. Read the sentences. Find the verb in each one. Write it on your paper.

1. The band is practicing now.
2. Cathy was practicing her flute.
3. Soon Thomas will be practicing the drums.
4. Sam has been practicing for thirty minutes.
5. Janet has been practicing the trumpet.
6. The band will have been practicing for an hour.

■ **Learn the different forms of the verb "be" so that you can write the progressive forms correctly.**

(To) **Be**

SIMPLE TENSES

Present	Past	Future
I am	I was	I will be
you are	you were	you will be
he is	he was	he will be
we are	we were	we will be
you are	you were	you will be
they are	they were	they will be

PERFECT TENSES

Present Perfect	Past Perfect	Future Perfect
I have been	I had been	I will have been
you have been	you had been	you will have been
he has been	he had been	he will have been
we have been	we had been	we will have been
you have been	you had been	you will have been
they have been	they had been	they will have been

ACTIVITY 2. Copy these sentences. Use the correct form of the verb *be* in each space.

1. I have _____ on an airplane six times.

2. Jack will _____ going to Seattle next week.

3. Doris has _____ in my class every year.

4. By noon today Mac will have _____ working for four hours.

5. Sara _____ leaving for Florida on Friday.

ACTIVITY 3. Write a correct sentence for each of the verbs below.

1. will have been going
2. has been working
3. had been eating
4. is beginning
5. was writing
6. were whispering
7. am opening
8. am moving

ACTIVITY 4. Use each verb below in a sentence in the tense shown in the parentheses. Do yours like this example:

pass   (present progressive)
Fred *is passing* Allen the butter.

1. drive   (future progressive)
2. have   (past progressive)
3. fish   (present progressive)
4. see   (future perfect progressive)
5. pour   (past perfect progressive)
6. go   (simple past)
7. wonder   (present perfect progressive)
8. play   (simple future)
9. hurry   (simple present)
10. jump   (present perfect)

ACTIVITY 5. Write the tense of each underlined verb phrase.

1. Martin had never gone to Texas before.
2. He is flying there for a vacation.
3. He will be leaving at noon.
4. Martin has been packing all morning.
5. His father called for him.
6. They are going to the airport now.

ACTIVITY 6. In each of these sentences the participle form of the verb is missing. Copy the sentence on your paper. In the space, write the correct word from the parentheses. Read the examples first.

- Use the present participle (verb + -ing) with the helping verb "be."
  Vera *is fixing* her bike.
- Use the past participle form (verb + -ed) with the helping verb "have."
  Vera *has fixed* her bike.
- If the verb phrase includes "have" and "be," use the present participle.
  Vera *has been fixing* her bike.

1. Janet has been _____ the trumpet for several years. (playing, played)
2. She has _____ in the Wilson band for two years. (playing, played)
3. This year the band is _____ to Florida for a national contest. (going, gone)
4. Some of the parents will be _____ the band. (accompanying, accompanied)
5. The band members have been _____ money. (raising, raised)
6. So far they have _____ more than one thousand dollars. (raising, raised)
7. In the fall everyone is _____ Christmas cards. (selling, sold)
8. So far, they have _____ a thousand boxes. (selling, sold)
9. Janet herself has _____ two boxes. (buying, bought)
10. She will be _____ cards soon after Thanksgiving. (addressing, addressed)

LESSON REVIEW. Write a sentence using the verb "sharpen" in each of the six regular tenses and the six progressive forms. "Sharpen" is a regular verb.

1. present — Fred *sharpens* his pencil before class.
2. past
3. future
4. present perfect
5. past perfect
6. future perfect
7. present progressive
8. past progressive
9. future progressive
10. present perfect progressive
11. past perfect progressive
12. future perfect progressive

Now, read the paragraph below. List the verb or verb phrase in each sentence. Write the tense beside each.

   Louis Armstrong played the trumpet. He earned a special place in American history. As a child he was living in an orphanage in New Orleans. There he first studied the cornet. In 1922, he had been playing on a Mississippi riverboat. He joined a band in Chicago. Then in 1924, Armstrong moved to New York City. Soon he was playing the trumpet. He invented a completely new style. By 1925, he was recording his music. Later he had formed his own band. People also loved his husky voice. In the 1930's, Armstrong was starring in movies. His popularity continued for the rest of his life. One of his records, "Hello, Dolly!" sold two million copies in 1964. Armstrong died in 1971. People will remember the man and his music for a long time.

LESSON FOUR. THE EMPHATIC FORM—THE VERB WITH "DO" OR "DID"

The helping verbs "do" and "did" are used to emphasize the negative word.

Many stores *do* **not** *close* on holidays. (present)

Dan *did* **not** *find* his book. (past)

The helping verbs "do" and "did" are used to form questions.

Do you like strawberries? (present)

Did you finish that book? (past)

The helping verbs "do" and "did" are used only with the present form of the main verb.

Did you *go* home? (The verb "go" is present.)

The emphatic form is used only to express present and past tense.

I *do* not *want* to be late for lunch. (present)

Frank *did* not *find* his coat. (past)

■ **The verb "to do" is also used as a main verb.**
The main verb *do* means "to perform an action."

Brigette *does* her chores early. (present)

Victor *did* his work well. (past)

Everyone *will do* his part. (future)

The family *has done* its work. (present perfect)

We *had done* the yard work. (past perfect)

Soon he *will have done* his lessons. (future perfect)

ACTIVITY 1. Find all the verbs and their helpers in these sentences. List them on your paper.
  1. Did you see Cathy at lunchtime?
  2. Jack never did find his gloves.
  3. The family is doing the dishes.
  4. Do you read the newspaper?
  5. Where do you do your homework?

ACTIVITY 2. Decide whether "do" is a helping verb or a main verb in each sentence below. Do yours like this example:

Soon he <u>will have done</u> his report.
will have done — *main verb*

  1. After dinner Ted and Janet <u>did</u> the dishes.
  2. Finally they <u>had done</u> their chores.
  3. Janet <u>had</u> already <u>done</u> her homework.
  4. "<u>Did</u> you <u>see</u> my math book?" Ted asked.
  5. "You <u>are</u> always <u>doing</u> something with that book!" Janet laughed.
  6. "I <u>did</u> not <u>see</u> it today," he said.
  7. At last Ted <u>did find</u> the book.
  8. Soon he <u>was doing</u> his math.

LESSON REVIEW. Write the verb and any helper for each sentence. Then identify the tense.
  1. In the fall people <u>do</u> extra yard work.
  2. <u>Did</u> you rake your leaves yet?
  3. They have already raked their yard.
  4. Does your family plant grass seed in the fall?
  5. Soon they will have done the whole yard.
  6. I have already done my part.
  7. Did Dad do the front yard yet?
  8. The boys are doing their part.
  9. They did not trim the trees this year.
  10. Did you find all of the verbs?

LESSON FIVE. THE CONDITIONAL FORMS

> Some helping verbs put a condition on an action. A condition is a requirement or a responsibility.
>
> **May-Might**   — He *may succeed.*
>   He *might succeed.*
>
> **Can-Could**   — He *can sing.*
>   He *could sing.*
>
> **Shall-Should**   — You *shall leave.*
>   You *should leave.*
>
> **Will-Would**   — The basket *will hold* a bushel.
>   He *would like* that movie.
>
> **Must**   — I *must go* now.
>   You *must find* your paper.
>   They *must leave* quickly.
>
>   Now, look carefully at the main verbs in the verb phrases above. They are all present tense verbs.
>
>   **Helping Verb**   +   **Present Tense**
>   may   succeed
>   will   hold

ACTIVITY 1. Read these sentences. Find the verb phrases. List them on your paper.

1. You may stay there until ten o'clock.
2. Janet can play the trumpet.
3. The basket will hold a dozen tomatoes.
4. She should do her homework.
5. She must finish her report tonight.

■ The conditional helping verbs are irregular. Do NOT add an -s to the verb when you use it with a singular subject.

Singular Subject	Plural Subject
He *may* go.	They *may* go.
Jack *must* leave.	The men *must* leave.

■ All of the other regular verbs and irregular verbs DO either add an -s or change to a different form.

Singular Subject	Plural Subject
He *sings* well.	They *sing* well.
He *has* gone.	They *have* gone.
She *is* going.	They *are* going.

ACTIVITY 2. Copy these sentences on your paper. Use the correct word in the parentheses in the spaces.

1. Every day Andy _____ at the gym. (exercise, exercises)
2. They _____ every day. (exercise, exercises)
3. Ted _____ exercise today. (might, mights)
4. He would _____ every day if he had time. (goes, go)

■ The conditional form may be combined with the compound tenses.

Present Perfect Tense	— I *have* gone.
Conditional Form	— I *could have* gone.
	— He *might have* gone.

Present Progressive Form	— I *am* going.
Conditional Progressive	— I *could be* going.
	— They *must be* going.

ACTIVITY 3. List the verb phrase in each sentence on your paper.

1. Janet's purse will hold many things.
2. She should clean it up.
3. In fact, she must clean it up.
4. She cannot find anything in it.
5. Janet should have bought a new purse.
6. She might be buying a new one.
7. Should she buy a new purse?

■ **In some sentences, the main verb is not included. It is understood.**

Are you doing your homework?

No, but I *should*. (The phrase "do my homework" is understood.)

LESSON REVIEW. Find the verb or verb phrase in each sentence. Write each one on your paper.

1. Next week, I might be going to Indiana.
2. I could have gone last year.
3. This year I must go.
4. I would like to leave Monday.
5. I should pack my suitcase.
6. I must take my winter coat.
7. I can go there by plane.
8. I may take only one suitcase.
9. Should I take a raincoat?
10. It might rain.

LESSON SIX. ACTIVE AND PASSIVE VERBS

> A verb is active if the subject is doing the action.
>
> Carlos *wrote* a story.
>
> A verb is passive if something happens to the subject.
>
> The story *was written* by Carlos.
>
> To form the passive verb, use the helping verb *be* with the past participle.
>
> **Right:** The story was written by Carlos.
>
> **Wrong:** The story was wrote by Carlos.

ACTIVITY 1. Find the verbs in the sentences below. Decide whether each verb is active or passive. Write your answers on your paper.

1. John Steinbeck wrote many stories.
2. *The Red Pony* was written by John Steinbeck.
3. Edgar Allan Poe wrote many poems.
4. "The Raven" was written by Poe.
5. That cake was baked by my aunt.
6. My aunt baked that cake.

ACTIVITY 2. Use each verb in two sentences. First, use it as an active verb, then as a passive verb.

1. cover
2. direct
3. discover
4. disturb
5. grease

6. hit
7. invent
8. cook
9. answer
10. pack

■ **In some sentences, part of the idea is missing. The missing part is "understood."**

The verbs in the examples below are passive.
The person who did the action is not named.

Today the bank *was robbed.* (by someone)
The pass *was thrown well.* (by someone)

ACTIVITY 3. Read these sentences. Find the verbs and their helpers. Write them on your paper.

1. America was discovered by Columbus.
2. We were disturbed by a loud noise.
3. The telephone was finally answered.
4. The ball was hit to left field.
5. The car was greased last month.

LESSON REVIEW. Read each sentence. Write the verb and any helper on your paper.

1. The cotton gin was invented by Eli Whitney.
2. Cotton seeds are removed from the cotton.
3. In 1842, the Oregon Trail was explored by John Fremont.
4. Fremont was later elected as one of California's first senators.
5. *Gone With the Wind* was written by Margaret Mitchell.
6. Her book was made into a successful movie.
7. Indiana was settled in 1808 by Tecumseh, an Indian leader.
8. Tecumseh was killed at the battle of the Thames in Canada during the War of 1812.
9. In 1848, Lewis Cass was defeated by Zachary Taylor.
10. Taylor was chosen as president of the United States.

LESSON SEVEN. VERBALS—VERBS USED AS NOUNS AND ADJECTIVES

A *verbal* is a verb form that is used as a noun or an adjective in a sentence. There are three kinds of verbals: the participle, the gerund, and the infinitive.

PARTICIPLES

■ **A participle is a verb form used as an adjective.** It describes a noun or a pronoun.

The *barking* dog made everyone angry.

(The participle *barking* describes the noun *dog*.)

GERUNDS

■ **A gerund is a verb form used as a noun.**

Skiing is a popular winter sport.

(The gerund *skiing* is the name of an activity.)

INFINITIVES

■ **An infinitive is a verb form made up of the word "to" plus the verb.** It is usually used as a noun, but may be used as an adjective or adverb, as well.

We like *to fish* in the lake.

(The infinitive *to fish* names an activity.)

ACTIVITY 1. List each participle below on your paper. Next to each, write the noun it describes.

1. The blaring stereo gave us a headache.
2. The police chased the speeding car.
3. The creaking door was broken.

ACTIVITY 2. List the gerunds on your paper.
1. Janet likes playing in the band.
2. James enjoys playing on the football team.
3. Dieting helped Anne lose ten pounds.
4. Whistling is helpful when you are scared.

ACTIVITY 3. List the infinitives on your paper.
1. We always like to study in the library.
2. They like to go to the beach.
3. The team wanted to win the game.
4. To graduate from college was Ted's goal.

ACTIVITY 4. List the verbs in these sentences. Do not include the verbals.

Janet wanted to find a new winter coat.

wanted   (*To find* is an infinitive.)

1. Janet went shopping with Darleen.
2. They hoped to find some coats on sale.
3. Shopping soon made them hungry.
4. Their growling stomachs gave them the message.
5. They looked for a place to eat.
6. Later they decided to go home.
7. Walking had made them tired.

LESSON REVIEW. List five verbals in these sentences. Then identify each one. It will be a participle, gerund, or an infinitive.

1. Fishing is something that we like to do.
2. The singing waiters brought our food to us.
3. Finding verbals is not hard to do.

CHAPTER REVIEW

The purpose of this chapter was to help you do two things:

1. Find the action verbs or verb phrases in sentences.
2. Use action verbs correctly.

Now, find out how much you understand.

Part 1. List the verbs or verb phrases that are in these sentences. Do not include verbals.

1. George Herman Ruth began playing baseball in 1914.
2. His teammates gave him the nickname "Babe."
3. He first played with the minor league Baltimore Orioles.
4. Baltimore sold his contract to the Boston Red Sox.
5. Babe pitched and batted left-handed.
6. He won many games as a pitcher.
7. In 1919, he broke all of the records for home runs in a season.
8. The New York Yankees had been looking at Ruth.
9. In 1920, he was sent to the Yankees.
10. He would play in more games in the outfield.
11. He continued to lead the league in home runs for many years.
12. He was hitting more home runs every year.
13. In 1927, he would set a new record.
14. He had hit sixty home runs in a single year.
15. In his last game, Babe Ruth hit three home runs in a row.
16. He was elected to the Baseball Hall of Fame in 1936.

Part 2. Read each sentence carefully. Choose the correct word in the parentheses for each one. List the words on your paper.

1. Mr. Jones _____ to work. (went, gone)
2. The Wildcats will _____ their first game on Saturday. (play, played)
3. The team _____ every day. (practice, practices)
4. They _____ a victory. (want, wants)
5. Everyone _____ to win. (like, likes)
6. He _____ never had an injury. (have, has)
7. They have _____ two touchdowns. (score, scored)
8. Monday they _____ to work. (hurryed, hurried)
9. Last week the man _____ at the trial. (testifies, testified)
10. I have _____ my work. (beginned, begun)
11. He _____ his lunch every day. (bring, brings)
12. Yvonne _____ the answer. (knowed, knew)
13. Sara always _____ her work well. (do, does)
14. The band _____ practicing now. (is, are)
15. The children _____ riding their bikes. (is, are)
16. He _____ flying to Florida. (be, is)
17. Did you _____ that book? (finish, finished)
18. Did Juan _____ home yet? (go, went)
19. He _____ go home now. (must, musts)
20. Jane _____ be finished by noon. (is, could)
21. The book was _____ by Jack London. (wrote, written)
22. That cake was _____ by Bob. (bake, baked)
23. The electric light bulb was _____ by Thomas Edison. (inventing, invented)
24. We _____ disturbed by the bell. (was, were)
25. The barking dog _____ everyone angry. (make, made)

5

The State-of-Being Verbs

> A state-of-being verb tells something about the condition or state of the subject of the sentence.

■ **The most common state-of-being verb is "to be."**

James *is* a tackle.

He *was* on the team last year.

Other state-of-being verbs include *appear, feel, look, taste,* and *become.*

■ **State-of-being verbs also express tense.** They may have helping verbs.

Present	— Leroy *looks* happy.
Past	— The water *felt* warm.
Future	— She *will be* sixteen soon.
Present Perfect	— He *has been* there before.
Past Progressive	— They *were being* nice.
Conditional	— She *could be* late.

WARM-UP 1. Find the verb or verb phrase in each sentence below. Write it on your paper.

1. My aunt is eighty years old.
2. She is looking well.
3. She also has felt healthy.
4. Aunt Marie is a good cook.
5. She has been keeping very active.

(State-of-being verbs that are also linking verbs are presented in Chapter 12, page 225.) 101

■ **"To be" is always a state-of-being verb when it is the main verb of the sentence. Some other state-of-being verbs can have more than one meaning. They may express a state of being or an action.**

Action Verb — Michael *tasted* the stew.
State-of-Being Verb — The stew *tasted* good.

WARM-UP 2. Decide whether the verb in each sentence expresses action or a state of being. Write your answers on your paper.

1. Howard finally *appeared* on the field.
2. He *appears* strong and healthy.
3. I *felt* the soft cloth.
4. The cloth *felt* nice to me.
5. She *looked* everywhere for Tiny.
6. Tiny *seemed* lost.
7. The oak tree *grew* eight feet.
8. I *grow* radishes in my garden every year.

WARM-UP 3. Find the mistake in each sentence. Copy the sentences correctly on your paper.

1. George be very tall and strong.
2. Donna and George is in the same class.
3. Donna thinks that George seem nice.
4. They was late to class one day.
5. "Be on time is important," the teacher said.

Now you are ready to begin the lessons in Chapter 5. You will do three things:

1. Find the state-of-being verbs in sentences.
2. Tell the difference between action verbs and state-of-being verbs.
3. Use state-of-being verbs correctly.

LESSON ONE. WHAT IS A STATE-OF-BEING VERB?

A state-of-being verb tells something about the condition of the subject of the sentence. It does not tell *what* the subject is doing.

State-of Being Verb —James *is* on the football team.

Action Verb —James *plays* on the football team.

In the first sentence, the verb *is* helps to make a statement about James. In the second sentence, the verb *plays* tells us the action that James does.

A state of being is the situation or condition of someone or something. The verb *to be* is the most common state-of-being verb. *To be* means "to exist, to live, or to happen."

Here are some other state-of-being verbs:

appear	grow	seem
become	look	smell
feel	keep	stay
get	remain	taste

ACTIVITY 1. Use only state-of-being verbs to make five statements about James. Here are some examples.

He *seems* nice.

He *is* a student.

He *grew* tall.

He *gets* taller every year.

He *looks* friendly.

ACTIVITY 2. Look at the picture below. Complete the statements in the column on your right. The verbs are in italics. Write the entire sentences on your paper.

1. The mountains *are* . . .
2. The scene *seems* . . .
3. The deer *appears* . . .
4. The lake *may be* . . .
5. The cloud *is* . . .
6. The water probably *tastes* . . .
7. The air *smells* . . .
8. The lake *looks* . . .
9. The trees *grow* . . .
10. The mountains *remain* . . .

ACTIVITY 3. Remember that a state-of-being verb does not tell us what the subject is doing. It does not express action. Read the sentences below. Decide whether each underlined verb expresses action or a state of being. Write your answers on your paper.

1. The Jones family <u>is</u> in the den.
2. Mrs. Jones <u>is reading</u> a book.
3. Ted <u>is</u> asleep on the sofa.
4. He <u>seems</u> tired this evening!
5. Mr. Jones <u>stays</u> awake.
6. He <u>is eating</u> an apple.
7. He <u>likes</u> a snack in the evening.
8. Janet <u>appears</u> very busy.
9. She <u>must be doing</u> homework.
10. The television <u>is</u> on.

The verb "to be" is the most common of the state-of-being verbs. Remember that "to be" is also a helping verb. It is used with a main verb to express progressive form.

Janet *is cooking* dinner.

She *is being* helpful.

Remember that "to be" is also used to form passive verbs. "To be" is a helping verb in those verb phrases, too.

The picture *was painted* by Norman Rockwell.

Dinner *is cooked* by Janet on Mondays.

ACTIVITY 4. Find the verbs or verb phrases in the sentences below. List them on your paper. Tell whether the verb "to be" is a main verb or a helping verb in each sentence.

1. Dawn was feeling fine yesterday.
2. Today she is sick.
3. She is going to the doctor.
4. Dawn will be absent from school.
5. She will probably be fine tomorrow.
6. Dawn was given some medicine by the doctor.

■ **State-of-being verbs also express tense.**

Present	— The water *feels* warm.
Past	— He *looked* good yesterday.
Future	— Mary *will be* fifteen next week.
Present Perfect	— I *have been* hungry all day.
Past Perfect	— Jack *had seemed* tired.
Future Perfect	— Carol *will have been* on her diet for a month tomorrow.

ACTIVITY 5. Find the verb or verb phrase in each sentence. Then identify the verb tense.

1. "The Tell-Tale Heart" is an interesting story.
2. Sam will not be here today.
3. Mrs. Frances has been in that room for two years.
4. She was a Spanish teacher.
5. I had been to New York twice before.
6. We will have been there a long time.

■ **State-of-being verbs may be used in the progressive form.** Use the verb "to be" as a helping verb. Then use the present participle form of the verb.

> He *is being* nice today.
> Carol *had been looking* good all week.
> I *will be feeling* fine soon.

ACTIVITY 6. Write the present participle for each state-of-being verb below. Then use each verb in a sentence, as in this example:

grow — *growing*   I *am growing* taller this year.

1. be   4. look
2. seem   5. feel
3. appear   6. become

■ **Conditional helping verbs may be used with state-of-being verbs.**

> Karl *must be* in love.
> I *could be* there at noon.
> You *should look* your best tomorrow.
> Anne *should have been* at the party.

ACTIVITY 7. Each of the sentences below has a state-of-being verb as the main verb. Find the verb or verb phrase. Write each one on your paper.

1. Ted and Janet were ready for Thanksgiving.
2. The turkey would taste good.
3. The pumpkin pies in the oven smelled enticing.
4. Everything looked delicious.
5. "Is dinner ready yet?"
6. The whole family was hungry.
7. "I have been hungry all day!"
8. Finally dinner was ready.
9. It is not a moment too soon for me.

LESSON REVIEW. Read these sentences carefully. Find the verb or verb phrase in each one. Write it on your paper. Beside each verb or verb phrase, write the word *action* or *being*. Do yours like the examples.

>She tasted the pie. *tasted — action*
>Dinner will be ready soon. *will be — being*

1. Dinner was served at three o'clock.
2. The food looked wonderful.
3. "Dinner is looking especially good today."
4. "I want the drumstick!"
5. The sweet potatoes tasted excellent.
6. "I will have more of the corn."
7. Mrs. Jones looked pleased.
8. "I am getting full."
9. Tomorrow they will probably all be on a diet.
10. All too soon the meal was over.

LESSON TWO. ACTION OR STATE OF BEING?

The verb "to be" is always a state-of-being verb when it is the main verb in a sentence.

The turkey *is* golden brown.

Many other state-of-being verbs can also be used as action verbs.

Janet *tasted* the cranberry sauce.

The cranberry sauce *tasted* sweet.

In the first sentence, *tasted* expresses action. Janet did something. In the second sentence, *tasted* expresses a state of being. The condition of the cranberry sauce was sweet.

In this lesson you will study the different uses of several state-of-being verbs.

APPEAR

action — to come into view; to become visible

Jack *appeared* in court.

The actor *appeared* in the play.

being — to seem; to look

They *appear* friendly.

Fred *appears* taller than Mike.

ACTIVITY 1. Write whether the underlined verb in each sentence expresses action or a state of being.

1. Lana suddenly appeared at the party.
2. She appeared to have a good time.
3. Mrs. Frances appears friendly.
4. Yvonne had appeared in court before.

FEEL

action — to touch; to think or believe
She *felt* the soft blanket.
I *feel* that you are right.

being — to be aware of a physical or mental
sensation
I *feel* cold.
Harvey *feels* happy.

GROW

action — to cause to grow; to cultivate
I *grew* tomatoes in my garden.

being — to come into existence; to spring up
Don *grew* two inches this year.
Orchids *grow* in Hawaii.

SMELL

action — to catch the scent or odor of something
I *could smell* the breakfast bacon.

being — to have a certain scent or odor
The bread *smells* fresh.

ACTIVITY 2. Write *action* or *being* for each verb.
1. She could <u>smell</u> the smoke in the air.
2. The warm cake <u>smelled</u> inviting.
3. The oven <u>felt</u> too hot.
4. Mary <u>felt</u> the hole in her pocket.
5. Joe <u>grows</u> orange trees in Arizona.
6. She has <u>grown</u> as tall as I.
7. Our cat <u>smells</u> his food before he tastes it.
8. Andy <u>felt</u> wonderful about his perfect score.

If you are not sure if a verb is a state-of-being verb, try this test. Substitute the verb "be" for the verb. If the meaning of the sentence is almost the same, the verb is a state-of-being verb. You cannot substitute "be" for an action verb.

Being Verb — They *remained* friends. (or)
They *were* friends.

Action Verb— He *got* a new job.
He *was* a new job. (not possible)

ACTIVITY 3. Use each verb below in two sentences. In one sentence, let the verb express action. In the other, it should express a state of being.

appear	feel	grow	look
taste	get	keep	smell

LESSON REVIEW. List the verb or verb phrase in each sentence. Decide whether it expresses action or a state of being. Write your answers on your paper.

1. Mr. Jones was looking for the newspaper.
2. He usually keeps it on the coffee table.
3. That paper gets harder to find every day.
4. Suddenly the newspaper appeared!
5. There it was on the table.
6. The newspaper appeared wrinkled.
7. It also looked torn.
8. "Who got this paper first?"
9. Mr. Jones grew angry for a moment.
10. Then he relaxed.
11. The newspaper was not damaged too much.
12. He remained in his chair with his newspaper for a while.
13. He got the news of the day.

LESSON THREE: USING STATE-OF-BEING VERBS

A state-of-being verb must agree with its subject. Regular verbs and most irregular verbs add an -s to the present form when the subject is singular.

Singular Subject	Plural Subject
Jack *looks* happy.	They *look* happy.
Mike *feels* rested.	They *feel* rested.

The past form of the verb stays the same for singular and plural subjects.

Singular Subject	Plural Subject
Donna *looked* nice.	Both girls *looked* nice.
She *felt* wonderful.	They *felt* wonderful.

The verb "to be" is an EXTREMELY irregular verb. Whether it is a main verb or a helping verb, its form changes several times.

Singular	Present	Past
First Person	I am	I was
Second Person	you are	you were
Third Person	he is	he was
Plural		
First Person	we are	we were
Second Person	you are	you were
Third Person	they are	they were

ACTIVITY 1. Complete these exercises on your paper.

1. Name all of the present forms of "to be."
2. Name all of the past forms of "to be."
3. The third person singular pronoun has three forms: masculine, feminine, and neuter. Name those three pronouns.
4. What forms of "to be" can be used with the third person singular subject?
5. Write a sentence using the verb "was."

■ The past participle of "to be" is "been." Use "been" with "have," "has," and "had" to form the perfect tenses.

> Fred *has been* there before.
> They *have been* away for a week.
> Mike *had been* there for two days.

■ The present participle of "to be" is "being." Use "being" with the helping verb "to be" to show the progressive form.

> Donna *is being* nice.
> Jack *was being* friendly.

ACTIVITY 2. Use the correct form of the verb "to be" in these sentences. Copy them on your paper.

1. Gail _____ a cheerleader this year.
2. Alice's report _____ due yesterday.
3. They _____ all at a party last week.
4. Have you ever _____ to Yellowstone Park?
5. Yellowstone Park _____ in Wyoming.
6. The children were _____ silly.
7. "You _____ next," the nurse said.
8. I had never _____ to Columbus, Ohio before.

■ Use the verb "be" to show future tense and to show simple conditional forms.

Future — He *will be* home soon.
Conditional — Janet *must be* late.

ACTIVITY 3. Use the correct form of the verb "to be" in these sentences. Copy them on your paper.

1. Will you _____ at the meeting today?
2. I should _____ on time.
3. Must I always _____ the first one?
4. Can I _____ the last one?
5. Howard will _____ at practice today.

Here are some common mistakes to avoid:

1. Sometimes people are careless and leave out the "be" verb or part of the verb phrase in a sentence.

    Wrong: The quarterback fast!
    Right: The quarterback *is* fast!
    Wrong: I *be* ready soon.
    Right: I *will be* ready soon.

2. Sometimes people use the infinitive form of the "be" verb (without the "to") instead of the correct present form.

    Wrong: They *be* good friends.
    Right: They *are* good friends.

    Wrong: James *be* in my class.
    Right: James *is* in my class.

ACTIVITY 4. Find the mistake in each sentence. Write the sentences correctly.

1. "Where James?" Darleen asked.
2. "He be at football practice," Sam said.
3. "They be practicing late today," she said.
4. "We be going to the drugstore after school."
5. "He be here soon," Sam told her.

■ **The infinitive "to be" is not part of the verb or verb phrase. It is often used after the main verb.**

> Donna appeared *to be* happy.
> Sam seems *to be* taller than Fred.
> I want *to be* the captain of the team.
> Donna tried *to be* friendly.

LESSON REVIEW. Copy these sentences on your paper. Write the correct form of the verb "to be" in each space.

The Beauty Contest

1. In November there will _____ a contest at Wilson High School.
2. Janet _____ entering the contest.
3. She wants to _____ "Miss Wilson High."
4. Her talent _____ playing the trumpet.
5. Sixty other girls _____ in the contest.
6. On the night of the contest, Janet's parents _____ there.
7. Andy _____ in the front row.
8. Before the contest, Janet had _____ nervous.
9. When she came on stage to play her trumpet, she _____ calm.
10. Later she had to _____ in an evening gown.
11. She _____ wearing a bright red dress.
12. "Who will _____ the winner?" everyone wondered.
13. Finally the judges announced the winner. Janet _____ "Miss Wilson High."
14. Mr. and Mrs. Jones _____ very proud.
15. So _____ Andy.

16. Janet _____ the happiest of all!

CHAPTER REVIEW   Subj. + Verb

Part 1. Find the verb or verb phrase in each sentence. List all of them on your paper.

1. The last days of November grew cold.
2. Winter winds felt chilly.
3. The days were growing shorter.
4. The sky became dark early in the evening.
5. The cool air smelled fresh and clean.
6. On most days the sky was clear.
7. There was little rain that fall.
8. Soon the first snowfall would come.
9. Everyone was feeling full of energy.
10. It was a pleasant time of the year.

Part 2. Decide whether the verb or verb phrase in each sentence expresses action or a state of being. Write your answers on your paper. Write Verb + A or B

1. The weather in December stayed cold.
2. People got out their winter coats.
3. "It gets cold earlier every year," Ted complained.
4. One day the sky looked gray.
5. "I can smell snow in the air," said Andy.
6. "It feels too cold to snow," Ted said.
7. "Hey! I felt a snowflake," said Andy.
8. They looked in Ted's garage for his sled.

Part 3. Copy these sentences on your paper. Use the correct form of the verb "to be" in each.

1. "It definitely _____ snowing," Andy said.
2. "I _____ ready to go skiing," Ted said.
3. "So, now you _____ happy about the snow!"
4. Soon the snow _____ deep enough.
5. Ted and Andy _____ sledding on a nearby hill.
6. They had _____ sledding for an hour.
7. They should _____ going home for dinner.
8. "I will _____ back soon!" said Andy.

Chapter 6

The Adverb

> An *adverb* is a word that answers questions about, or modifies, a verb, an adjective, or another adverb.

■ **An adverb answers questions about the action or the state of being expressed in a sentence.**

Questions	Examples
How?	Mr. Jones drives *carefully*.
When?	The football game is *tomorrow*.
Where?	Janet is studying *upstairs*.

■ **An adverb also answers questions about an adjective or another adverb. These adverbs are called adverbs of degree.**

Questions	Examples
How bright?	A dolphin is *extremely* bright.
How small?	I had a *very* small lunch.
To what degree?	The winds howled *very* loudly.

WARM-UP 1. Find the adverbs in these sentences.

1. You should read the sentences carefully.
2. Adverbs are hidden everywhere.
3. The weather was very cold yesterday.
4. You are making too much noise.
5. I was almost asleep.
6. Darleen threw Tiny's old collar away today.

■ **"Never" and "not" are adverbs of negation.**
A negative word means the action will not happen or
the state of being is not present. The adverb "not" is
often hidden in a contraction.

> She is *never* home.
> Tiny won*'t* eat his dinner. (will not)
> They did*n't* find the book. (did not)
> Carol is *not* at school today.

WARM-UP 2. Copy these sentences on your paper.
Circle the adverbs of negation.
1. There is not enough snow to ski.
2. Fred couldn't find his pencil.
3. It was not his fault.
4. I have never met him.
5. They had never been there before.

■ **Adverbs can be used to make comparisons.** They
are used much like adjectives. The words "more" and
"most," and "less" and "least" are adverbs of degree.
They are often used to compare adjectives or other
adverbs.

Positive	Comparative	Superlative
fast	faster	fastest
slowly	more slowly	most slowly
quickly	less quickly	least quickly
well	better	best

WARM-UP 3. For each sentence write the correct
form of the adverb which is in parentheses.
1. Of all the girls, Donna runs _____ . (fast)
2. Howard works _____ than Jim. (slowly)
3. Beth sings well, but Dan sings _____ . (well)
4. When I am tired, I work _____ than when I am
    rested. (quickly)

Now, you are ready to begin Lesson One.

LESSON ONE. ADVERBS THAT MODIFY VERBS

> Adverbs that answer the question, HOW? are usually used with action verbs. They tell us something about the way the action was done.
>
> Tiny barked *loudly*.
> They did the assignment *correctly*.
> Jack guessed *right*.
> Carol works *fast*.

ACTIVITY 1. Copy these sentences on your paper. Add an adverb that answers the question, "How was the action done?" The verb is in italics.

1. The family *ate* their dinner . . .
2. Willis *drives* his car . . .
3. May *sews* . . .
4. *Read* these sentences . . .
5. Mrs. Jones *sang* . . .
6. We *cleaned* the house . . .

ACTIVITY 2. In each sentence, find an adverb that answers the question, "How?" Write the adverbs on your paper.

1. The ballerina danced gracefully.
2. The acrobat climbed the ladder carefully.
3. Laura helped us gladly.
4. Slowly Joyce found the answers.
5. James played the game hard.
6. Janet plays the trumpet well.
7. The farmer planted the corn quickly.
8. I got home fast.
9. We went on vacation happily.
10. She sewed the hem straight.

Adverbs also answer the questions, WHEN? HOW OFTEN? HOW LONG? or HOW MANY TIMES? They tell something about the time of the action or state of being.

I am leaving town *today*.
Janet will be home *soon*.
I would like to go to the beach *again*.
John will speak *next*.
Carol is *usually* happy.

ACTIVITY 3. Use each of these adverbs in a sentence. Underline each adverb. When

1. often	7. now
2. tomorrow	8. always
3. never	9. later
4. still	10. twice
5. yesterday	11. already
6. today	12. again

ACTIVITY 4. Each of these sentences has an adverb that tells something about the time of the action or state of being. List these adverbs on your paper.

1. Please begin immediately! When
2. I'd like to go first.
3. They jumped up instantly.
4. That was a long time ago.
5. I saw the movie before.
6. The weather has been nice lately.
7. Sometimes I enjoy golf.
8. Occasionally we visit our relatives in Texas.
9. The newspaper is delivered daily.
10. We trim our trees yearly.

Adverbs also answer the question, WHERE? or IN WHAT DIRECTION? They tell something about the place of the action or state of being.
Tiny lives *there*.
Leave your coat *downstairs*.
You should turn *left*.

ACTIVITY 5. Each sentence below has an adverb that tells something about the place of the action or state of being. List these adverbs on your paper.

1. The team advanced the ball forward. *Where*
2. Please go away.
3. Turn right at the corner.
4. Hang your coats here.
5. The bedrooms are upstairs.
6. They looked at the stars above.
7. The storm seems to be near.

LESSON REVIEW. Read these sentences carefully. Find all of the adverbs. List them on your paper. A sentence may have more than one adverb.

Where *When* *How*

1. Yesterday Tiny carelessly lost his bone. (2)
2. He barked loudly at Darleen. (1)
3. "You are always losing your things!" Darleen (2) scolded him angrily.
4. "I will never buy you anything again!" (2)
5. Tiny jumped up and down constantly. (3)
6. He would not stop barking. (1)
7. Finally Darleen found the bone. (1)
8. She gave it to Tiny quickly. (1)
9. Tiny ran away with it happily. (2)
10. "Be careful with it now!" she scolded. (1)

LESSON TWO. ADVERBS OF DEGREE

Adverbs that answer questions about adjectives and other adverbs are called adverbs of degree. They answer the questions, HOW MUCH? HOW LITTLE? HOW OFTEN? and TO WHAT DEGREE?

In the example below, the adverb "very" tells us about the adjective "cold."

In the example below, the adverb "extremely" tells us about the adverb "fast."

ACTIVITY 1. Copy these sentences on your paper. Circle the adverbs of degree.

1. Tiny is very careless.
2. He barks too much.
3. He makes everyone so angry!
4. He is an unusually noisy dog.

■ **The adverb of degree is usually placed before the adjective or adverb.**

ACTIVITY 2. Read these sentences. The underlined word is an adjective. Find the word that tells about the adjective. Write the word on your paper.

1. I am almost <u>ready</u> to go.
2. Fred was rather <u>happy</u> today.
3. That coat is too <u>small</u> for you.
4. Mrs. Edwards was quite <u>pleased</u> with the class.
5. They were completely <u>satisfied</u> with their new stove.
6. The extremely <u>strong</u> wind blew down the tree.

ACTIVITY 3. Read these sentences. Now the underlined word is an adverb. Find the word that tells about that adverb. Write it on your paper.

1. Read these sentences very <u>carefully.</u>
2. Alice works too <u>quickly.</u>
3. The band played unusually <u>well.</u>
4. I am leaving sometime <u>today.</u>
5. Please go far <u>away.</u>
6. Donna left much <u>later</u> than Yvonne.
7. Carl swims somewhat <u>often.</u>

ACTIVITY 4. Copy these sentences on your paper. Add an adverb of degree before the adjective or adverb that is underlined. Use a different adverb of degree in each sentence.

1. The <u>strong</u> man lifted five hundred pounds.
2. Victor is <u>ready.</u>
3. Your new sweater is <u>pretty.</u>
4. Sally does her work <u>well.</u>
5. Anne plays tennis <u>often.</u>
6. Lon works <u>quickly.</u>

ACTIVITY 5. Use each of these adverbs of degree in a different sentence. Underline the adverb.

1. very
2. too
3. quite
4. rather
5. somewhat

6. extremely
7. unusually
8. completely
9. so
10. almost

LESSON REVIEW

Part 1. Read these sentences. Find the adverbs of degree. List them on your paper.

1. Ted enjoyed his job at Mr. Jackson's store very much.
2. Mr. Jackson was completely satisfied with Ted's work.
3. Ted worked extremely hard.
4. "You are an unusually good worker," Mr. Jackson said.
5. "You can expect a very nice raise next month."
6. Ted was quite pleased to hear that!

Part 2. In each of these sentences, find the adverb or adjective. Copy the sentences on your paper. Add an adverb of degree to each one.

1. December is a cold month.
2. People must dress warmly.
3. Many of the trees are bare.
4. The skies may be cloudy.
5. Soon we will have snow.
6. I will be ready to go shopping tomorrow.

LESSON THREE. RECOGNIZING ADVERBS

Sometimes people are not sure whether a word is an adjective or an adverb. Let's review the definitions of those two parts of speech.

- **An adjective describes a noun or pronoun.**
Nancy is *tall*. (*Tall* describes Nancy.)
Nancy is a noun; therefore, *tall* is an adjective.
- **An adverb answers a question about a verb in a sentence.**
Nancy lives *there*. (*There* tells us where Nancy lives.)
Lives is a verb; therefore, *there* is an adverb.

ACTIVITY 1. List the underlined words in these sentences. Next to each, write whether it is an adjective or an adverb.

1. Larry is <u>late</u>.
2. He is <u>here</u>.
3. That house is <u>large</u>.
4. She works <u>hard</u>.
5. He is a <u>hard</u> worker.
6. Jack lives <u>here</u>.
7. <u>Today</u> we jogged.
8. We arrived <u>late</u>.
9. They arrived <u>later</u>.
10. We <u>usually</u> eat at noon.
11. He runs <u>fast</u>.
12. He's a <u>fast</u> runner.
13. He is <u>fast</u>.
14. The answer is <u>clear</u>.
15. Speak <u>clearly</u>!
16. We shower <u>daily</u>.
17. Do <u>daily</u> exercises.
18. Let's go <u>early</u>.
19. Is this the <u>early</u> show?
20. We looked <u>up</u>.

■ **Many adverbs are made from adjectives by adding the ending -ly.**

Adjectives	Adverbs
The cloth is *soft*.	He sang *softly*.
The candy is *sweet*.	She smiled *sweetly*.
Carol looks *happy*.	Fred laughed *happily*.

ACTIVITY 2. Write each underlined word. Tell whether it is an adjective or an adverb.

1. The sea was very <u>calm</u> today.
2. Donna walked <u>calmly</u> out of the room.
3. Between classes the halls were <u>quiet.</u>
4. The kangaroo <u>quietly</u> watched the people.
5. "This is an <u>extremely</u> difficult case," the lawyer said.
6. "This is an <u>extreme</u> case," the lawyer said.
7. Fred is always <u>hungry.</u>
8. The people ate lunch <u>hungrily.</u>

■ **Sometimes an adverb is made from a noun by adding -ly.**

Noun	Adverb
May I have *part* of that?	He is *partly* finished.

ACTIVITY 3. Write each underlined word. Tell whether it is a noun or an adverb.

1. The books were in alphabetical <u>order.</u>
2. Please do things <u>orderly.</u>
3. We went to the store every <u>week.</u>
4. The family shops <u>weekly.</u>
5. The bills arrive every <u>month.</u>
6. We pay our bills <u>monthly.</u>

■ **Not all words ending in -ly are adverbs. Many common adjectives end in -ly, too.**

Ted received some *fatherly* advice from Mr. Jones.
Donna is usually *friendly*.

ACTIVITY 4. Is the underlined word in each sentence an adjective or an adverb? Write your answers on your paper.

1. New cars are very costly.
2. Strychnine is a deadly poison.
3. That is an ugly cut.
4. They sat quietly and waited.
5. Donna's report was timely.

■ **Some words that end in -ly are used as either adjectives or adverbs.**

Adjectives	Adverbs
He did the *daily* report.	He reported *daily*.
We left in the *early* morning.	We left *early*.

LESSON REVIEW. On your paper, identify the part of speech for each underlined word. List the words and write either "adjective" or adverb" next to each.

1. We fed the rats a deadly poison.
2. Mr. Jones prepared his yearly report.
3. We receive a newspaper daily.
4. Please try to come to class early.
5. Darleen smiled happily.
6. Where have you been lately?
7. I am partly finished with my report.
8. They went to Chicago on the early train.
9. We listened to the daily weather report.
10. "The shoes this year are ugly," Janet said.

LESSON FOUR. COMPARING WITH ADVERBS

Many adverbs are used to make comparisons. The three degrees are *positive, comparative,* and *superlative.*

Positive	Comparative	Superlative
fast	faster	fastest
slowly	more slowly	most slowly
happily	less happily	least happily
well	better	best

One-syllable adverbs form their comparative and superlative forms by adding -er and -est. Adverbs of more than one syllable usually form their comparative and superlative forms by using "more" and "most" and "less" and "least," which are adverbs of degree. A few adverbs are irregular, such as "well," "better," and "best."

Remember to use the comparative form to compare two things. Use the superlative form to compare more than two things.

Donna finished *more quickly* than Ben.

Tom worked *most quickly* of them all.

ACTIVITY 1. On your paper, write the adverbs below.

1. This shoe fits comfortably.
2. This shoe fits more comfortably than that one.
3. This shoe fits most comfortably of all.
4. Victor is speaking calmly.
5. He is speaking more calmly than George.
6. He speaks most calmly when he has practiced his speech.
7. Jack writes well.
8. He writes better this year.
9. He writes best about football.

ACTIVITY 2. Write each adverb below on your paper. Then write the comparative and superlative forms next to each, as in this example:

softly — *more softly, most softly*

1. loudly
2. brightly
3. fast
4. hard
5. gladly
6. clearly
7. softly
8. angrily

ACTIVITY 3. Copy these sentences. Fill in the correct form of each adverb in parentheses.

1. The lights shone _____ . (brightly)
2. Carol sings _____ than Fred. (well)
3. Dan works _____ when he is interested. (hard)
4. Of all the students, Kim worked _____ . (quickly)
5. Zeke played the trumpet _____ than Janet. (loudly)

LESSON REVIEW. Find the adverbs and list them on your paper. Write the degree of comparison beside each, as in this example:

Sara dances most unusually.
most unusually — *superlative*

1. Paul runs the mile faster than Sam.
2. Everyone in class worked hard.
3. I work best when I am rested.
4. Carl reads less quickly than Mike.
5. The choir sang the chorus more loudly than the verse.
6. Everyone worked least happily at the end of the day.
7. I like chocolate better than vanilla.
8. The winds howled most loudly at midnight.
9. The children played more quietly after lunch.
10. Janet plays the trumpet well.

LESSON FIVE. USING ADVERBS CORRECTLY

In a statement the tense of the verb and the adverb of time must agree.

Wrong: Jack sings next.
Right: Jack will sing next.

(*Next* suggests that the action will happen in the future.)

Wrong: Tomorrow we go to work.
Right: Tomorrow we will go to work.

(*Tomorrow* is future time; therefore, the verb should be future tense.)

ACTIVITY 1. In the sentences below, the adverbs of time are underlined. Verbs are in parentheses. Write the correct tense of the verb for each sentence.

1. We _____ there a year <u>ago.</u> (go)
2. <u>Yesterday</u> we _____ late to class. (be)
3. Sally _____ <u>soon.</u> (arrive)
4. We _____ the house <u>before.</u> (paint)
5. Tiny _____ his dinner <u>now.</u> (eat)

■ **Always use an adverb in a sentence when answering a question about a verb.**

ACTIVITY 2. Choose the correct word in parentheses after each sentence. Write it on your paper.

1. Carol dances _____ . (graceful, gracefully)
2. Fred laughed _____ . (happy, happily)
3. The winds howled _____ . (loud, loudly)
4. Give me that _____ ! (quick, quickly)
5. Sit there _____ ! (quiet, quietly)

■ Use "good" and "well" correctly.

Good is always an adjective. Never use *good* to answer questions about a verb.

Right: We had a good day.
Wrong: They worked good together.

Well is sometimes an adverb. *Well* means to do something correctly.

Right: She speaks well.
Wrong: She speaks good.

Good and *well* can both be used after state-of-being verbs. In the sentence below, *well* is an adjective.

Right: I feel good today.
Right: I feel well today.

ACTIVITY 3. Copy these sentences. Write either *good* or *well* in each space.

1. Carol is _____ at arithmetic.
2. Dan dances very _____ .
3. She did her _____ deed for the day.
4. Mike always does his work _____ .
5. Gail isn't feeling _____ today.

LESSON REVIEW. Copy the sentences on your paper. Correct the mistake in each one.

1. Yesterday we are late to class.
2. Please finish that work quick.
3. Janet plays the trumpet very good.
4. Between Fred and Mike, Fred drives best.
5. "Shhh! Sara spoke now," said the teacher.
6. Anne always talks very soft.

CHAPTER REVIEW

In this chapter, your goal was to recognize adverbs in sentences. An adverb answers questions about verbs, adjectives, and other adverbs. The questions are HOW? WHEN? WHERE? HOW MUCH? HOW OFTEN? and TO WHAT DEGREE?

Read these sentences. Find all of the adverbs. List them on your paper in order. A sentence may have more than one adverb.

1. A heavy snowfall arrived early in December.
2. Most of the people at Wilson High School were very happy.
3. The teachers and students waited somewhat patiently.
4. They were expecting an announcement that school would be dismissed early.
5. At home Ted was not so pleased.
6. He had to go to work anyway.
7. He knew the roads would be extremely slippery.
8. Mr. Jackson's store never closed for snow.
9. The store would probably be very busy.
10. The store was having an unusually good sale on ski jackets.
11. Ted drove more slowly that day.
12. Finally he arrived at work.
13. He walked across the parking lot carefully.
14. The store was almost empty.
15. The other salespeople were talking excitedly about the snow.
16. The day passed quickly.
17. Soon it was time for Ted to leave.
18. "I still have time to go sledding," he thought to himself.
19. He found Janet already outside.
20. "Hey! I'm here!" he called to her.

Prepositions and the Prepositional Phrase

A *preposition* is a word that shows a relationship between a noun or pronoun and another part of the sentence.

A preposition is a part of a phrase. Look at these examples:

down the street	*for* him
at the movies	*under* the table
in the middle	*on* the table

The first word in the phrase is the *preposition*. The last word is the noun or pronoun. The noun or pronoun is called the *object* of the preposition.

Preposition   Object

We walked *through* the woods.

WARM-UP 1. Read these sentences. Find the prepositional phrases and write them on your paper.

1. Tiny saw another dog across the street.
2. The dog was sleeping under a tree.
3. Tiny barked at the dog.
4. Then he dashed down the sidewalk.
5. He tried to play with the other dog.

■ **A prepositional phrase acts like an adjective or an adverb.** Look at the examples below.

Adjective Phrases

The house *across the street* is for sale.
(Which house? The one across the street.)

The book *by Judy Blume* was popular.
(Which book? The one by Judy Blume.)

Adverb Phrases

Ted works *in the evenings*.
(When does Ted work? In the evenings.)

Please report *to the office*.
(Report where? To the office.)

WARM-UP 2. Read these sentences. The prepositional phrases are underlined. Decide if the phrase is an adjective or adverb. Write your answers on your paper.

1. The letter from Mary arrived yesterday.
2. The music of Brahms was played at the concert.
3. Ted and Andy both go to Hanover Community College.
4. Janet is a student at Wilson High School.
5. The gift from my aunt arrived before Christmas.
6. During the winter we like to ski.
7. Tiny chased a cat up a tree.
8. A girl in my class wrote a short story.
9. She sent the story to a magazine.
10. The day after tomorrow is my birthday.

■ Some words can be either a preposition or an adverb. A preposition has an object. An adverb does not.

Preposition — She looked *up* the street.
Adverb — Jack looked *up.*

WARM-UP 3. Read these sentences. Decide whether the underlined word is a preposition or an adverb. Write your answers on your paper.

1. Please come in.
2. Howard walked in the woods.
3. Turn the lights off when you leave.
4. Jane jumped off the stage.
5. I will come by tomorrow.
6. Sam lives by the lake.
7. Mike came over to see us last night.
8. Tiny jumped over the fence easily.

■ Prepositional phrases make sentences more interesting.

WARM-UP 4. Add at least one prepositional phrase to each sentence below. Do yours like the example. Be sure to add only prepositional phrases.

The boy arrived.
The boy *from Texas* arrived *in the evening.*

1. My aunt wrote me a letter.
2. The janitor helped the students.
3. My neighbor got a new car.
4. The quarterback threw the ball.
5. The crowd cheered.

Now you are ready to begin Lesson One.

LESSON ONE. UNDERSTANDING PREPOSITIONS

A preposition expresses a relationship between one part of a sentence and another word. That word is called the object of the preposition. Look at the examples below.

Jan received a *letter* from *Mary*.

What is relationship between the *letter* and *Mary*?

The letter is *from* Mary.

Jan wrote a *letter* to *Mary*.

Now what is the relationship between *letter* and *Mary*?

The letter is *to* Mary.

ACTIVITY 1. Copy each of these sentences on your paper. Write a word in the space that expresses a relationship between the two words in italics.

1. The *apples* ___ the *tree* are ripe.
2. The *house* ___ the *corner* is Jack's.
3. The *story* ___ *Edgar Allan Poe* was written in 1838.
4. The *girl* ___ the *picture* is my sister.
5. The *coat* ___ the *chair* is mine.
6. The *star* ___ the *movie* was John Wayne.
7. The *dessert* ___ *whipped cream* tasted best.
8. The *man* ___ the *beard* arrived late.
9. The *girl* ___ *Ken* is a good dancer.
10. The *picture* ___ the *wall* is my favorite.

■ **Each preposition has a certain meaning.**

ACTIVITY 2. Under each picture below there is a sentence. The preposition is missing. Copy the sentence on your paper. Add a preposition that expresses the relationship shown in the picture.

1. Janet is ___ Darleen.

2. The birds are ___ the water.

3. Tiny is ___ the table.

4. Tiny is ___ the table.

5. Ted is ___ the house.

6. James is ___ Janet and Darleen.

ACTIVITY 3. Here is a list of some commonly used prepositions. Write a sentence using each one. Underline the whole prepositional phrase. Do yours like the example.

aboard — Fred is <u>aboard the ship.</u>

1. about	8. behind	15. in	22. over
2. above	9. beneath	16. into	23. past
3. across	10. beside	17. near	24. through
4. after	11. down	18. of	25. to
5. around	12. during	19. off	26. under
6. at	13. for	20. on	27. until
7. before	14. from	21. out	28. with

■ A preposition must have an object. The object is a noun or pronoun.

Preposition + object = prepositional phrase

■ The object is a noun or pronoun. A noun often has adjectives before it.

across *the muddy* field

■ Because adverbs answer questions about adjectives, a prepositional phrase may also contain an adverb.

after the (very) long meeting

■ Usually when the object of the preposition is a pronoun, the prepositional phrase will be only two words — the preposition and the object.

to him   for her   beside it

ACTIVITY 4. Read these sentences. Find the prepositional phrases. Copy them on your paper.

1. We bought our groceries at the store.
2. Here is a list of sentences.
3. We looked across the clear blue lake.
4. We lived near a very busy highway.
5. Would you please sit here with me?
6. Write your name in the left-hand corner.
7. Give this book to him.
8. Around the corner lives my best friend.
9. I like apple pie with ice cream.
10. John Kelly was mayor of the city.
11. Did you vote for him?
12. James Polk was born in North Carolina.
13. Later Polk moved to Tennessee.
14. Susan walked home during a heavy storm.
15. Howard gave this gift to me.

■ **Some words can be used either as prepositions or as adverbs. A preposition has an object. An adverb does not.**

Jim looked *around*.

Around is an adverb. *Around* tells where Jim looked.

Jim looked *around* the corner.

Around is a preposition. *Around* expresses a relationship between the corner and the rest of the sentence.

ACTIVITY 5. Read each sentence. Decide whether the underlined word is a preposition or an adverb. Write your answers on your paper.

1. Darleen put Tiny <u>outside.</u>
2. Tiny barked <u>outside</u> the door.
3. Don't stay <u>outside</u> in the rain.
4. Put the cat <u>out!</u>
5. Turn the light <u>out</u> before you leave.
6. Quick! Come look <u>out</u> the window!
7. The rain was falling <u>down</u> heavily.
8. We drove the car <u>down</u> the highway.

ACTIVITY 6. Use each of the words below in two sentences. Use it first as a preposition. Then use it as an adverb.

1. in
2. on
3. below

4. up
5. underneath
6. inside

■ **There are also compound prepositions.** Here are some examples.

according to	in spite of
because of	instead of
in addition to	out of
in front of	as far as
in place of	along with

ACTIVITY 7.   Find the compound preposition in each sentence.   Write the whole prepositional phrase on your paper.

1.   According to Joe, the party was fun.
2.   I am going instead of Tim.
3.   Vic will speak in place of Judy.
4.   Please get the dog out of the house.
5.   Randy will go along with us.
6.   Donna is in front of Karl.

LESSON REVIEW.   Read these sentences. Find all of the prepositional phrases.   Make a list of them on your paper.

1.   Ted was studying for his final exams.
2.   He stayed in his room and studied.
3.   Andy called him on the telephone.
4.   "I need some help from you," he said.
5.   Andy lived around the corner.
6.   He arrived in ten minutes.
7.   "It is math again," he said. "It is just too tough for me."
8.   They studied together for several hours.
9.   The next day Andy went to class.
10.   In spite of his troubles, Andy passed the test.
11.   "I couldn't have done it without your help," he told Ted.

LESSON TWO. THE PREPOSITIONAL PHRASE USED AS AN ADJECTIVE

The prepositional phrase is usually used in a sentence either as an adjective phrase or as an adverb phrase. In this lesson you will study the adjective phrase.

An adjective is a word that describes or defines a noun or pronoun. A prepositional phrase can be used as an adjective. Look at the examples below.

Adjective — The *middle* girl is Jean.

Prepositional Phrase — The girl *in the middle* is Jean.

The prepositional phrase used as an adjective does the same thing as an adjective. The phrase tells *which one*, *what kind*, or *how many*.

You will notice that the adjective usually comes before the noun. The prepositional phrase comes after the noun.

ACTIVITY 1. The underlined words in these sentences are prepositional phrases. Find the word that each phrase is describing. Write it on your paper. Do yours like the example.

What kind <u>of car</u> is that?
kind

1. Andy's homework <u>in math</u> was difficult.
2. The boy <u>with me</u> is my cousin.
3. The flowers <u>on the table</u> are beautiful.
4. We built a house <u>of brick</u>.
5. None <u>of the girls</u> left early.
6. All <u>of the people</u> applauded.
7. The poem <u>by Emily Dickinson</u> was lovely.

■ When you write, **you** decide whether to use an *adjective* or a *prepositional phrase*. Look at the examples. Both sentences have the same meaning.

Adjective — The *Wilson High* team won.

Prepositional Phrase — The team *from Wilson High* won.

ACTIVITY 2. Rewrite each of these sentences. Change the adjective in italics to a prepositional phrase.

1. *John Steinbeck's* story was exciting to read.
2. Darleen bought *football* tickets.
3. It was a beautiful *spring* day.
4. We chose a lovely *diamond* ring.
5. I bought a *city* map.
6. The *porch* light needed a new bulb.
7. Those are *ski* boots.
8. The *kitchen* table is new.
9. Carol's *English* homework was easy.
10. We built a *brick* house.

■ A prepositional phrase can describe the object of another preposition.

The man *at the end of the line* is Mr. Jones.

(*At the end* describes *man*; *of the line* tells about *end*.)

ACTIVITY 3. Find all of the prepositional phrases in these sentences. Write them on your paper.

1. We walked in the woods beside the lake.
2. Ted works in a store in Marshall Mall.
3. We went to Yellowstone Park in Wyoming.
4. Put this on the table in your room.
5. All of the people in the auditorium cheered.

■ **Prepositional phrases used as adjectives make sentences more interesting.**

ACTIVITY 4. Rewrite these sentences. Add a prepositional phrase after each noun or pronoun.

1. Everyone likes the football games.
2. Several people are coming to the party.
3. The books fell off the shelf.
4. The library closed at noon.
5. The man bought a new car.
6. The teacher liked that book.

LESSON REVIEW. Find the prepositional phrases in these sentences. List them on your paper. After the phrase write the word it is describing. Do yours like the example.

> The pen on Frank's desk has no ink.
> on Frank's desk — *pen*

1. Alaska in January is very cold.
2. The beautiful spruces throughout the state are snow-covered.
3. Janet studied the history of Alaska.
4. Vitus Bering was the first explorer of Alaska.
5. People from Russia also explored there.
6. The Russians made their headquarters in Sitka.
7. Now Alaska is a state in the United States.
8. Alaska is one of our last frontiers.
9. The population of Alaska is very small.
10. Janet enjoyed her study of Alaska.

LESSON THREE. THE PREPOSITIONAL PHRASE USED AS AN ADVERB

> An adverb is a word that answers questions about a verb. A prepositional phrase can also be used as an adverb. Look at the examples below.
>
> **Adverb** — We shopped *rapidly.*
>
> **Prepositional Phrase** — We shopped *in a hurry.*
>
> The prepositional phrase used as an adverb does the same thing as an adverb. The phrase tells us HOW we shopped.

ACTIVITY 1. The prepositional phrase in each sentence is an adverb phrase. Decide what question the adverb phrase is answering about the verb. On your paper, write *How, When,* or *Where* for each sentence. Look at the example first.

Put the book on the table. — *Where*

1. I will be there in a minute.
2. Darleen ran up the stairs.
3. Andy and Ted drove to the lake.
4. The report was written before midnight.
5. Shakespeare was born in 1564.
6. We are going to Florida.
7. Make the pudding with milk.
8. Janet ironed her dress with great care.
9. The roast is in the oven.
10. Write your paragraph in ink.
11. Karl took his car to the garage.
12. Mr. Jones drives on Route 50 every day.
13. They went to the beach last summer.
14. She did her work with a smile.
15. Park the car in the garage.

■ **A prepositional phrase also answers the question WHY?** Look at the example below.

Janet bought a gift *for her mother.*
WHY did Janet buy the gift?

ACTIVITY 2. Each of these sentences has an adverb phrase. The phrase tells WHY something was done. List the adverb phrases on your paper.

1. I took an umbrella because of the rain.
2. Janet wrote a paper for English class.
3. Mrs. Jones made dinner for her family.
4. She bought an onion for the salad.
5. Ted bought a car for himself.
6. Please do something for me.
7. Andy took an aspirin because of his fever.

■ **A prepositional phrase used as an adverb answers a question about the verb. The phrase may tell something about the conditions of the action.**

Darleen went there *with Janet.*

Darleen was "with Janet" when she went there.

ACTIVITY 3. Find the prepositional phrases in these sentences. They will all be used as adverbs. A sentence may have more than one prepositional phrase. Write them on your paper.

1. Put the paper in the trash can.
2. The office is on the first floor in the building.
3. She was with her mother at the store.
4. Carol shopped for the family's groceries.
5. The firefighters saved the family from the fire.

■ An adverb may answer questions about an adjective or another adverb. A prepositional phrase used as an adverb can also tell something about an adjective or adverb.

Fred is now taller *by three inches.*

HOW MUCH taller is Fred? He is taller by three inches. The prepositional phrase tells something about the adjective *taller.*

In the race, Dan ran faster than Jack *by eight seconds.*

HOW MUCH faster than Jack did Dan run? He ran faster by eight seconds. The prepositional phrase tells something about the adverb *faster.*

ACTIVITY 4. Write these sentences on your paper. Add a prepositional phrase which answers a question about the underlined word. Do yours like the example.

I <u>saw</u> Tim.
I saw Tim *at school.*

1. Sally weighs <u>more</u> than Cathy.
2. Zeke <u>walks</u> every day.
3. They <u>arrived·</u>
4. Janet <u>took</u> her coat.
5. Ted <u>drove</u> his car.
6. The winds <u>blew</u> very hard.
7. Bob got the <u>highest</u> grade on the test.
8. We <u>visited</u> my aunt.
9. Please <u>fix</u> dinner.
10. Frank <u>did</u> his homework.

Prepositional phrases are often used as adverbs. An adverb answers a question about the verb. Remember that the prepositional phrase begins with a preposition. It ends with a noun or pronoun.

LESSON REVIEW. Find the prepositional phrases in these sentences. List them on your paper in order.

1. Andy is a student at Hanover Community College.
2. He will study computer technology for two years.
3. He will also take courses in accounting.
4. Someday Andy may work in a bank.
5. Computer workers are in almost every industry.
6. The first computers were installed in business firms in 1951.
7. Now, almost every business uses computers for recordkeeping.
8. At school, Andy loads computers with diskettes or tapes.
9. He watches the screen for information.
10. Andy is also learning about computer languages.
11. A computer programmer works with computer languages.
12. The programmer writes directions for the computer.

13. So far, Andy enjoys his work with computers.
14. He hopes to have a good job in the field.

LESSON FOUR. THE OBJECT OF THE PREPOSITION

The object of the preposition is a noun or pronoun. Be sure that you do not confuse a prepositional phrase with an infinitive. Look at the examples below.

Infinitives — He wants *to leave* early.
He hopes *to have* a job.

Prepositional Phrases — Ted went *to the bank.*
Janet wrote a letter *to her aunt.*

The word after the preposition *to* in an infinitive is a verb. Remember that the object of the preposition must be a noun or pronoun.

ACTIVITY 1. Read each sentence. Decide whether the underlined words are an infinitive or a prepositional phrase. Write your answers on your paper.

1. Andy went to his class.
2. He likes to work with computers.
3. "Turn to page 8," the teacher said.
4. Andy began to read his lesson.
5. He wanted to ask the teacher a question.
6. He went to the computer to practice.
7. Ted sent a get-well card to his friend.
8. The girl ran to catch the bus.
9. People on the bus waved to her.
10. Janet talked to Darleen
11. They climbed to the top of a high hill.

ACTIVITY 2. Write five sentences using the preposition *to*. Decide whether *to* is part of a prepositional phrase or part of an infinitive in each of your sentences.

■ **The object of the preposition is often a pronoun. The pronoun must be in the objective case.** See the chart on page 33.

> **Wrong:**   She sat between Ted and *I*.
>
> **Right:**   She sat between Ted and *me*.

■ **When personal pronouns are used for subjects and objects, they often have different forms. Other pronouns, however, keep the same form.**

> **Subject** — *Everyone* was late.
>
> **Object**   — We fixed dinner for *everyone*.

■ **Possessive nouns and pronouns are NOT used as objects of prepositions.**

> **Wrong:**   Jack went home with *his*.
>
> **Right:**   Jack went home with *him*. OR
>
> Jack went home with *his friend*.

ACTIVITY 3. Read these sentences. Find the prepositional phrases. List them on your paper.

1. Darleen wanted to study with her friend.
2. The table was empty. I put my books on it.
3. Ted studied by himself.
4. We bought gifts for everyone.
5. They had to choose between them.
6. Jan asked, "May I have a salad with this?"

ACTIVITY 4. Copy these sentences on your paper. Correct any mistakes.

1. Please bring a coat for Jack and I.
2. Sam bought a soda for hisself.
3. Susan passed out paper to everyone's.
4. Between the two of those, I like the red sweater better.

■ **Remember that the infinitive and the gerund can be used as nouns in sentences. The infinitive and the gerund can be the object of a preposition.**

Infinitive as
Object of a Preposition   — He is about *to leave.*

Gerund as
Object of a Preposition   — I use these shoes for *running.*

ACTIVITY 5. Find the prepositional phrases in these sentences. Copy them on your paper.

1. I have no choice except to study.
2. We use a stove for cooking.
3. Ted is about to go now.
4. That song is good for dancing.
5. We get information by reading.

■ **The object of a preposition usually comes after the preposition. Sometimes, however, the preposition and its object are separated.**

Object   Preposition
What did you do that *for*?

ACTIVITY 6. Find the preposition and its object in each sentence. Write the whole phrase on your paper.

1. Whom are you talking about?
2. Whom are Howard and Tom with?
3. I found the pen which he was writing with.
4. Ted found the book which he was looking for.
5. That is what I was searching for.

ACTIVITY 7. Read the paragraph below. Find all of the prepositional phrases and list them on your paper. There are two infinitives which should not be on your list.

Have you ever heard of Mary Lyon? She was a pioneer in the education of women. Mary Lyon was born in 1797. She died in 1849. She taught in schools in New Hampshire and in Massachusetts. In those days, only rich women could get a good education. She raised money to begin a school for middle-class women. In 1837, she opened a school in Massachusetts. The name of the school was Mount Holyoke. There women studied about mathematics, science, and Latin. Mary Lyon had no goal except to teach. She won the love of everyone through her work. Mary Lyon wanted to give women confidence in themselves.

LESSON REVIEW. Find the prepositional phrases in these sentences. List them on your paper.

1. Andy hopes to have a job in a bank.
2. He likes to work with computers.
3. Andy had to study for a test.
4. He studied with Ted and Mike.
5. The teacher gave the test to everyone.
6. They had no choice except to concentrate hard.
7. They had prepared for the test by studying.
8. Andy made a mistake on his paper.
9. "What did I do that for?" he thought.
10. Finally, he was finished with the test.
11. He gave his paper to the teacher and breathed a sigh of relief.

CHAPTER REVIEW

- A preposition is a word that shows a relationship between a noun or pronoun and another part of the sentence.
- A preposition is part of a phrase.
- The prepositional phrase is used as either an adjective or an adverb.

Part 1. A prepositional phrase in each of these sentences is underlined. Decide whether it is used as an adverb or an adjective.

1. The dress <u>in the window</u> is on sale.
2. The letter <u>from Aunt Sue</u> arrived yesterday.
3. Carol waited <u>for the mail carrier</u>.
4. <u>In the spring</u> we plant a garden.
5. I mowed the lawn <u>for my neighbor</u>.
6. Mary Lyon began a school <u>for women</u>.

Part 2. Read these sentences. Find all of the prepositional phrases. List them on your paper in order.

1. Mike came to see me for a minute.
2. He arrived in a yellow sports car.
3. We invited him to stay for dinner.
4. Mother made pizza for everyone.
5. Later we all helped with the clean-up.
6. Then Mike was about to leave.
7. "Thanks for dinner," he said.

Part 3. Copy these sentences on your paper. Add at least one prepositional phrase to each one.

1. Everyone was happy.
2. The weather was good.
3. The family went out.
4. They came home.
5. The family was tired.

Chapter 8

Conjunctions—
Words That Connect

A *conjunction* is a word that connects parts of a sentence.

Words   — *Darleen* **and** *Janet* went to the game.
Spaghetti sauce needs *tomatoes, onions,* **and** *spices.*

Phrases   — The basketball team *got the ball* **and** *scored a goal.*

Sentences   — Andy looked at new cars, **but** they were too expensive.
He liked the big cars best; **however**, he wanted good gas mileage.

A conjunction also introduces groups of words called *subordinate clauses.* These clauses are like adverbs. They answer the questions *where, when, how,* and *why.*

<u>Because</u> *Shelley was late*, she missed the bus.
She had to walk <u>if</u> *she wanted to get to school.*

Some conjunctions come in pairs. Look at the example.

Neither Ted **nor** Andy caught a fish.

WARM-UP 1. Read these sentences. Find the conjunctions. List them on your paper.

1. The football team scored the touchdown and the extra point.
2. Would you like vanilla or chocolate pudding?
3. Jack will succeed if he keeps on trying.
4. I would like to go, but I am tired.
5. We missed school yesterday because it was snowing.
6. Carol likes hockey; however, she prefers tennis.
7. Either tea or coffee will be fine.
8. For my birthday I got not only skis but also ski poles.
9. Alice didn't know whether to laugh or cry.
10. Darleen, Janet, and James are in the same class.
11. Fran checked the book out, but Dan read it.
12. We bought meat, fruit, and milk at the store.
13. After the game was over, the school had a dance.
14. Unless you try harder, you will not win.

■ **Conjunctions may be used to connect several ideas into one sentence.**

Janet is in line.

Darleen is in line.

James is in line.

Others are in line.

Janet, Darleen, James, *and* others are in line.

WARM-UP 2. Rewrite these sentences. Use a conjunction to connect the ideas.

1. Paul bought a coat. He bought a scarf. He bought some gloves.
2. It rained on Monday. It rained on Tuesday.
3. Dan was absent. Carol was absent.

LESSON ONE. COORDINATING CONJUNCTIONS

In this chapter, you will work with the three kinds of conjunctions. First, you will read about coordinating conjunctions.

A *coordinating conjunction* connects words, phrases, or sentences that are equal. Equal means that they do not depend on each other to make sense.

Shoes **and** *boots* are on sale today.

You could also say:

Shoes are on sale today. (or)
Boots are on sale today.

Look at these examples.

Words   — Rich plays the *guitar* **and** the *trumpet*.

Phrases   — He ran *around the corner* **and** *out of sight*.

Sentences — I'd like to help you, **but** I'm busy.

Some of the most common coordinating conjunctions are listed below.

    and   but   or   for   nor   as well as

ACTIVITY 1. Find the coordinating conjunction in each sentence. Write it on your paper.

1. Eight and eight make sixteen.
2. All night the winds blew, and the snow fell.
3. The referee blew his whistle and stopped the game.
4. The actor sang well, but he could not dance.
5. I don't like tea or coffee.
6. I couldn't study, for I was so tired.

■ **A coordinating conjunction may connect two or more complete ideas.**

We can say: I don't like tea.

                      I don't like coffee.

We can also say: I don't like tea *or* coffee.

The words that are the same in both sentences are not repeated.

ACTIVITY 2. Connect the ideas in the following pairs of sentences, using conjunctions. Do yours like the example above. You may need to change the verb form.

1. Carol likes ice cream. Fred likes ice cream.
2. James plays football. James plays basketball.
3. Edgar Allan Poe wrote short stories. Edgar Allan Poe wrote poetry.
4. I grew tomatoes in my garden. I grew green beans in my garden.
5. Laura likes basketball. Laura likes hockey.

ACTIVITY 3. Rewrite each of these sentences into two sentences. Leave out the conjunctions. Do yours like the example below.

       We bought hamburgers and rolls.

       We bought hamburgers. We bought rolls.

1. I like milk or water with my dinner.
2. Fred hits well, but he cannot catch a ball.
3. Vic tried hard but couldn't make the team.
4. Poe wrote short stories as well as poetry.
5. After school we played records and relaxed.
6. John Adams and Thomas Jefferson were vice-presidents of the United States.
7. President Harry Truman was born in 1884 and died in 1972.

■ **Use a comma to separate words or phrases in a series. A series is more than two words or phrases.**

Janet, Darleen, and *Sue* arrived late.
We planted flowers *in the front, in the back,* and *on the sides* of the house.

Place the comma *after* the items in the series. Do not put a comma after the last item in the series.

ACTIVITY 4. Copy these sentences on your paper. Add commas only where they are needed. Circle the conjunctions.

1. We planted bushes trees and flowers around the the house.
2. We planted tulips daffodils and hyacinths.
3. Later we washed up changed our clothes and went out to dinner.
4. I ordered a hamburger french fries and milk.
5. For dessert we had a choice of ice cream pie cake or pudding.
6. The restaurant had vanilla ice cream but no strawberry.
7. They had apple cherry and peach pie.

ACTIVITY 5. Write a sentence using each of these conjunctions. Each sentence should have a series. Be sure to punctuate correctly.

1. and
2. but
3. or
4. nor
5. as well as
6. for

■ **Two or more sentences joined with a conjunction always need a punctuation mark.**

Use a comma to separate sentences joined with *and, but, nor, or, for.*

Ted dug up the garden, *and* Janet planted the seeds.

Our family doesn't like spinach, *nor* do we like squash.

Use a semicolon (;) when you connect sentences with these coordinating conjunctions:

besides	however	furthermore
accordingly	also	therefore
moreover	otherwise	consequently
nevertheless	instead	

Janet likes to play the trumpet; *however*, she doesn't always like to practice.

Fred worked all day; *nevertheless*, he didn't finish.

ACTIVITY 6. Copy these sentences on your paper. Punctuate them correctly.

1. Janet must hurry otherwise she will be late.
2. We wanted to go shopping instead we stayed home.
3. After dinner Janet read a book Ted did homework Mr. Jones watched TV and Mrs. Jones just relaxed.
4. Karl rode the bus to school but he walked home.
5. Tiny likes steak but all he gets is dog food.
6. The storm blew down several trees furthermore it damaged some telephone lines.
7. Poe wrote many short stories also he wrote some good poetry.
8. Roberto likes ice cream but his sister served pudding for dessert.

■ The words *but* and *for* can be used either as conjunctions or as prepositions.

Conjunction — Darleen feeds Tiny dog food, *but* Tiny prefers steak!

Preposition — No one was hungry *but* Tiny.

Conjunction — Randy brought the equipment, *for* he was the team manager.

Preposition — We knew that he would bring it *for* the team.

ACTIVITY 7. Read these sentences carefully. Identify the part of speech of the underlined word.

1. Paul played tennis well, <u>for</u> he practiced every day.
2. The new apartment was beautiful, <u>but</u> the rent was high.
3. Everyone liked the story <u>but</u> Yolanda.
4. The students cheered loudly <u>for</u> their team.

LESSON REVIEW. Copy these sentences on your paper. Add the necessary punctuation. Circle the coordinating conjunctions.

1. A new girl moved to the town where Janet and Darleen live.
2. Her name is Susan but everyone calls her Sue.
3. Sue was shy at first for she is deaf.
4. Janet and Darleen wanted to communicate with Sue better therefore they began to study sign language.
5. Soon they could use signs or finger spelling easily.
6. Sign language helped them "talk" to Sue furthermore it was fun!

LESSON TWO. SUBORDINATING CONJUNCTIONS

A *subordinating conjunction* connects clauses that are not equal. The clauses introduced by the subordinating conjunction depend upon the main clause to make sense.

A *clause* is a group of words with a subject and a verb.

The subordinate clause is a *dependent clause* because it cannot stand alone as a sentence. It is like an adverb. It answers the question *where*, *when*, *how*, or *why*. It may be at the beginning or at the end of the sentence.

After the party was over, we went home.

We went home *after* the party was over.

Here is a list of some commonly used subordinating conjunctions:

after	if	until	in order that
although	since	when	whenever
as	so	where	wherever
because	unless	while	

ACTIVITY 1. Find the dependent clause in each sentence. Write it on your paper. Include the subordinating conjunction.

1. If you are gaining weight, skip dessert.
2. I plan to study until I finish.
3. Harry's parents saved their money in order that he could go to college.
4. When Janet gets here, we will leave.
5. They ate popcorn while they watched the movie.
6. Newton is ten miles away as the crow flies.

■ **A dependent clause does not express a complete thought by itself.** Look at the example.

ACTIVITY 2. Add an independent clause (a sentence) to each of these dependent clauses.

1. Although Lassie is only a dog, . . .
2. Until the other team scored, . . .
3. Because my tooth aches, . . .
4. Since I flew on an airplane, . . .
5. When I finish this book, . . .

ACTIVITY 3. Now add a dependent clause to each of these sentences. Write the complete new sentence on your paper. Circle the subordinating conjunction.

1. Dan would like to visit California.
2. Karl saved five dollars a week.
3. My neighbors got a new dog.
4. Anne's report was always late.
5. The Jones family might buy a computer.

■ **Use a comma after the dependent clause only when it is at the beginning of the sentence.**

Comma — *Unless you hurry*, you won't finish.

No comma — You won't finish *unless you hurry.*

ACTIVITY 4. Connect each of these pairs of sentences with a subordinating conjunction. Punctuate your sentences correctly.

1. Zeke is lifting weights. He wants to be on the wrestling team.
2. Pete went to the library. He needed a book.
3. Sue is in Darleen's English class. She moved to town in March.
4. I was asleep. A storm blew down our tree.
5. You will drive today. I will drive tomorrow.

■ **Some words can be used either as subordinating conjunctions or as prepositions.**

Conjunction — The game stopped *because* it rained.

Preposition — The game stopped *because of* rain.

In the first example, *it rained* is a clause. It has a subject and a verb. In the second example, *rain* is the object of the preposition *because of.*

ACTIVITY 5. Read each sentence. Decide whether the underlined word is a conjunction or a preposition. Write your answers.

1. Donna went home <u>after</u> school.
2. We went home <u>after</u> school was over.
3. <u>Because of</u> Ted, we won the game.
4. I like that coat <u>because</u> it is warm.
5. I haven't heard from her <u>since</u> Monday.
6. I'll leave <u>since</u> you are here now.
7. <u>Before</u> class began, I talked to the teacher.
8. <u>Before</u> lunch, I have my French class.

ACTIVITY 6. Find the subordinating conjunctions in these sentences. List them on your paper.

1. We drove home carefully because it was snowing.
2. We had classes until noon although the weather was bad.
3. If the snow is deep enough, there will be no school tomorrow.
4. School is closed only when the snow is deep.
5. Where Janet and Ted live, there are usually two deep snows each year.

Lesson Review

Part 1. Connect each of these pairs of sentences with a subordinating conjunction. Punctuate the new sentence correctly. Be sure that your new sentence makes sense!

1. I made an A. I studied hard.
2. I will clean the house. You do the shopping.
3. I get hungry about three o'clock. I eat an apple.
4. The weather is too cold. I can't go outside.
5. He lost the election. He didn't get enough votes.

Part 2. Copy these sentences on your paper. Add the necessary punctuation. Circle the subordinating conjunctions.

1. Kathy won't fix dinner until everyone is hungry.
2. If you will help we can finish early.
3. When warm weather arrives Ted and Andy will go fishing.
4. Until the team scored the fans were quiet.
5. Everyone looked forward to warmer weather as spring approached.

LESSON THREE. CORRELATIVE CONJUNCTIONS

Correlative conjunctions are always used in pairs. Look at the example.

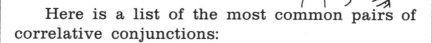

Neither Ted *nor* Andy enjoyed that movie.

Both the actors *and* the story were awful!

Here is a list of the most common pairs of correlative conjunctions:

neither . . . nor

both . . . and

not only . . . but (also)

either . . . or

whether . . . or

ACTIVITY 1. Read these sentences. Find the correlative conjunctions. Write them on your paper.

1. Darleen will write her report on either James Polk or Benjamin Harrison.
2. Both Polk and Harrison were U.S. presidents.
3. Not only Darleen but also Sue must write a report.
4. Neither Polk nor Harrison is very famous.
5. Sue doesn't know whether to write about Chester Arthur or Franklin Pierce.
6. She had heard of neither Arthur nor Pierce before.

■ **When subjects are joined with correlative conjunctions, the verb agrees with the subject nearest the verb.** Look at the examples.

Wrong: Neither Andy nor Ted *are* home yet.

Right: Neither Andy nor Ted *is* home yet.

Wrong: Not only the house but also the garage *need painting.*

Right: Not only the house but also the garage *needs* painting.

Wrong: Either candy or flowers *is* a nice gift.

Right: Either candy or flowers *are* a nice gift.

ACTIVITY 2. Choose the correct word in the parentheses to complete each sentence.

1. Either a pencil or a pen ____ satisfactory. (is, are)

2. Neither the coat nor the shoes ____ on sale. (is, are)

3. Neither the car nor the truck ____ working today. (is, are)

4. Not only Jack but also Gloria ____ running for class president. (is, are)

5. Either candy or perfume ____ a nice gift. (makes, make)

LESSON REVIEW. Find the correlative conjunctions in these sentences. Write them on your paper.

1. Both Ted and Andy have part-time jobs.

2. Sue takes neither cream nor sugar in her coffee.

3. Not only Darleen but also Tiny enjoys "Lassie."

4. Mr. Jones either drives to work or takes the bus.

5. Mr. Wiley must decide whether the reports are due on Monday or Tuesday.

CHAPTER REVIEW

Conjunctions are words that connect two or more words, phrases, or clauses in a sentence.

Part 1. Read these sentences. Find all of the conjunctions. List them on your paper.

1. Janet and Darleen were making plans for the Valentine's Day dance.
2. Darleen wondered whether James would ask her or not.
3. She decided to buy a new dress when she got her next paycheck.
4. Janet wanted to ask Andy, but she wasn't sure if he would go.
5. She also wasn't sure if Ted would approve.
6. After a few days passed, Janet got the courage.
7. "Either he will or he won't," she thought.
8. Andy did want to go, but he had a problem.
9. "I have neither money nor a good suit," he said.
10. "If you just wear slacks and a sports shirt, you will look fine," Janet told him.
11. "If it's that simple, I will go," said Andy.
12. Janet was pleased because he would be her date.

Come to the
VALENTINE'S DAY DANCE

Date: February 14th
Time: 8:00 P.M.
Place: Auditorium

Part 2. Copy these sentences on your paper. Add the necessary punctuation.

1. Janet Andy Darleen and James went to the dance together.
2. Because the car was small they were somewhat crowded.
3. While they were on their way they had a good time.
4. "If we don't get there soon we will miss the first dance," Darleen said.
5. "The dance committee wanted a band however they got a disc jockey," Janet said.
6. When they arrived they hurried to join their friends.
7. "Shall we dance or shall we check out the food?" Andy asked.
8. "Unless you're hungry let's dance," she answered.
9. The music was good and they had a wonderful evening.

Part 3. Copy these sentences on your paper. Fill in each space with a conjunction. There may be more than one correct answer.

1. _____ the dance, they went to a restaurant.
2. They were hungry, _____ they were not tired.
3. _____ James _____ Andy ordered hamburgers.
4. "I'm on a diet," said Janet, " _____ , I will have a milkshake."
5. They talked about the disc jockey _____ their friends.
6. _____ it was time to go home, they got back into the car.
7. Guess who was waiting _____ Andy took Janet to her door!
8. _____ were her parents there, _____ there was also Ted!

9

Interjections! Words That Express Feelings

An *interjection* is a word or phrase that expresses feelings. An interjection is not clearly related to the rest of the sentence. The interjection is a word that is "thrown in."

Here are some examples.

Oh, no! I forgot my money.
Ah, yes, this is terrific.
What? You don't know how to land?

Always separate the interjection from the rest of the sentence with a punctuation mark. You can use a comma, a question mark, or an exclamation point. Use an exclamation point after a strong interjection.

Hurray! We finally won the game.
Help! Fire! Please hurry!

WARM-UP. Read the sentence under each picture. Write the sentence on your paper. Add an interjection. Be sure to punctuate correctly.

Isn't that beautiful?

We're having a test.

That hurts.

I ripped my best shirt.

I won!

We're having liver.

Now you are ready to begin the lesson.

USING INTERJECTIONS

An *interjection* is a word or phrase that expresses a strong feeling. Always separate the interjection from the rest of the sentence with a punctuation mark. Look at the examples.

Oh, no! I'm late again.

Oh? I didn't know you were sick.

Hush. Everyone is working.

Say, could you help me?

Here are some other commonly used interjections.

Yes.	Whew!	Gosh.	Wow!
Hey!	What?	Ha!	Quick!
Ah.	Ouch!	Hurry!	Oh, boy.
Well.	My goodness!	So what?	Really?
Hello.	Nonsense.	Sorry.	Alas!

ACTIVITY 1. Make a list of ten different interjections. Include either words or short phrases. Use each one in a sentence. Be sure to punctuate correctly.

■ Capitalize the first word of the sentence after a mark of end punctuation such as a period, a question mark, or an exclamation point.

So? Who really cares?

Wow! That is lovely.

Whew. I'm glad I am finished!

■ You can also use a comma after an interjection. Do not capitalize the first word of the sentence that follows.

Ah, that dessert looks great!

ACTIVITY 2. Copy these sentences on your paper. Add punctuation after the interjections and at the end of the sentences. Capitalize the first words of sentences.

1. quick I need help fast
2. oh boy what a great car
3. really I didn't know that
4. well you finally got here
5. oh no you aren't giving me a shot

LESSON REVIEW. Look at each of the pictures below. Write a sentence about each one. Use an interjection in each one. Punctuate and capitalize correctly.

MASTERY TESTS FOR PART ONE

MASTERY TEST 1. Match each part of speech with its description.

1. Noun
2. Adjective
3. Pronoun
4. Verb
5. Adverb
6. Preposition
7. Conjunction
8. Interjection

a. It expresses action.
b. It connects words.
c. It names anyone or anything.
d. It expresses feelings.
e. It answers questions about a verb.
f. It describes a noun or pronoun.
g. It replaces a noun.
h. It expresses a relationship between a noun or pronoun and another part of a sentence.

MASTERY TEST 2. Identify the part of speech of each underlined word.

1. Janet and Darleen studied sign language.
2. They wanted to communicate with their new friend Sue.
3. They learned a sign for "I love you."
4. They learned both signs and finger spelling.
5. Each letter of the alphabet has a sign.
6. After they learned sign language, they taught other people.
7. "Say! Sign language is easy!" said James.
8. Sue was very pleased with her new friends.

"I love you."

MASTERY TEST 3. Copy these sentences on your paper. Capitalize the proper nouns and adjectives.

1. darleen has a french poodle named tiny.
2. tiny likes to eat swiss cheese.
3. My friend anne is learning spanish with her home computer.
4. We studied the indian tribes of new mexico.
5. karl enjoys his english and math classes.

MASTERY TEST 4. Copy these sentences on your paper. Add the necessary punctuation.

1. Because Darleen is Janets friend Janet bought her a birthday gift.
2. Sally bought four dollars worth of stamps but she needs more to mail the package.
3. That coat is Jacks and this one is yours.
4. Ouch That hurts.
5. Fred wanted to make the wrestling team therefore he lifted weights every day.

MASTERY TEST 5. Choose the correct word in the parentheses to complete each sentence.

1. Either milk or tea ___ fine with me. (is, are)
2. Neither Anne nor her friends ___ in the school band. (is, are)
3. Jim would like to go, ___ he is too busy. (and, but)
4. They planned to go fishing; ___ , it was too cold. (however, therefore)
5. The ___ tracks led under the baseboard. (mices, mice's)
6. Both of the ___ books were lost. (girl's, girls')
7. The store sold only ___ clothes. (ladys', ladies')
8. Henry the Eighth had six ___ . (wifes, wives)
9. Have you ___ dinner yet? (ate, eaten)
10. Everyone has already ___ home. (went, gone)

PART TWO:

SENTENCE PATTERNS

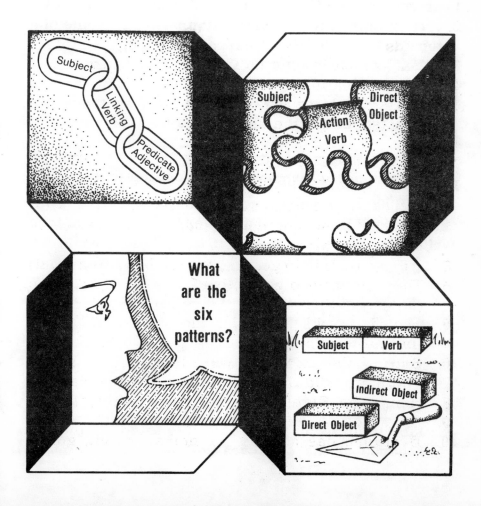

What Is a Sentence?

A sentence is a group of words that expresses a complete thought. A sentence may be very short. It may have only one word. Some of the ideas we wish to express are very simple. Other sentences may be very long because some of our ideas are complicated. The most important rule to remember about a sentence is that it should communicate an idea to another person.

■ **A sentence must express a complete idea.**

ACTIVITY 1. Here are some groups of words. Copy them on your paper. If the words form a sentence, write *Sentence* after them. If they do not, write *No.*

1. Stop!
2. Before the storm was over.
3. Across the street.
4. That's nice.
5. Every sentence expresses a complete idea.
6. Looking at new cars.
7. She laughed.
8. Jack thought that he would like to go fishing, but because of the cold weather he stayed home.

■ **A sentence has a subject and a predicate.** The subject names the person or thing that we are talking about. The predicate tells us what happened. The predicate always includes a verb.

ACTIVITY 2. Copy these sentences on your paper. Underline the subject once and the predicate twice. Look at the example below.

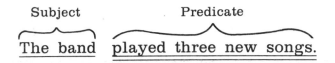

Subject   Predicate

The band played three new songs.

1. Andy is looking at new cars.
2. Everyone at the party had a good time.
3. Sue moved to town in March.
4. The whole family planned a party for Mrs. Jones.
5. They all helped.

■ **The subject is usually a noun or pronoun.** The words that describe the subject are part of the complete subject. We call the noun or pronoun the simple subject.

Simple subject — Sam's <u>car</u> had a flat tire.

Complete subject — <u>Sam's car</u> had a flat tire.

ACTIVITY 3. Copy these sentences on your paper. Underline the complete subject. Circle the simple subject.

1. Our neighbor painted his house.
2. His whole family picked out the color.
3. The color was brown.
4. They needed a ladder.
5. The part under the roof was hard to reach.
6. The whole job took them three days.

■ **The predicate part of a sentence tells us what happened.** The predicate always includes a verb. All of the words that tell about the verb are part of the predicate.

ACTIVITY 4.   Copy the predicate part of the sentence on your paper.   Circle the verb with all of its helpers. Look at the example below.

We rented a house at the beach.

(rented) a house at the beach

1. A popular band was coming to town.
2. Ted bought two tickets.
3. The concert was on Saturday evening.
4. He decided to take Sue.
5. Sue enjoyed music very much.
6. She could feel the vibrations of the band.

■ **A sentence can have more than one subject or predicate.** They are connected with conjunctions. We call them compound subjects or compound predicates.   Look at the examples.

Compound subject — *Ted and Sue* went to the concert.

Compound predicate — The band *sang and played.*

ACTIVITY 5. Copy the compound subjects or compound predicates on your paper.

1. Ted went to the auditorium and got the tickets.
2. Sue and Ted enjoyed the concert.
3. The band played their instruments and sang.
4. Both the band and the audience had a good time.

■ **A sentence can be simple, compound, or complex.**

Simple Sentence

A simple sentence has one subject and one predicate. The subject may be compound. The predicate may be compound. Look at the examples.

> Ted and Sue enjoyed the music.
> The band played well.

Compound Sentence

A compound sentence has two independent clauses joined together with a conjunction.

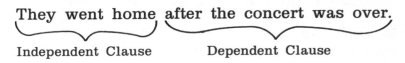

They left early, and they got home late.

Independent Clause   Independent Clause

Complex Sentence

A complex sentence has an independent clause and a dependent clause.

They went home after the concert was over.

Independent Clause   Dependent Clause

ACTIVITY 6. Read each of these sentences. Decide whether it is simple, compound, or complex. Write your answers on your paper.

1. I would like a hamburger.

2. The hamburger looks good, but I want the barbecue.

3. I can't give you a barbecue because we are all out of it.

■ **Every sentence has a purpose.** Sentences can make statements. They can ask questions. They can give commands or requests. Look at the examples.

Statement — They went to the concert.

Question — Did they go to the concert?

Command — Go to the concert.

Request — Please go to the concert.

• Any sentence can express strong feelings. It ends with an exclamation point to show those feelings.

Statement — The concert was really great!

Question — Did you see that car!

Command — Stop making that noise!

• A sentence which makes a statement usually begins with the subject.

The concert began at eight o'clock.

• A sentence which asks a question begins with either a helping verb or an interrogative pronoun or adverb.

Where are my shoes? *Are* you ready yet?

Who is she?   *Did* you like the music?

• A sentence which makes a command or request begins with a verb. The subject is understood to be the person we are talking to.

(You) Give me two tickets.

Give me two tickets.

BOX OFFICE

ACTIVITY 7. Read these sentences. What is the purpose of each one? Write one of these answers: *Statement, Question,* or *Command.*

1. Are you hungry?
2. Yes, I am.
3. Please order something.
4. I would like a milkshake.
5. What kind do you want?
6. I want a chocolate milkshake.
7. Wait just a second.
8. Here is your milkshake.
9. How much is it?
10. Look at the check.

■ **Sentences in our language follow patterns.** The pattern depends on the type of verb. There are two main kinds of verbs. They are *transitive* and *intransitive.*

A *transitive* verb has an object.

An *intransitive* verb does not have an object.

Transitive verb   Object   Intransitive verb

Sue *drank* the milkshake.   Then they *went* home.

ACTIVITY 8. The verb in each sentence is underlined. Decide whether it is transitive or intransitive.

1. Ted <u>drove</u> Sue to her home.
2. They <u>talked</u> about the concert.
3. Sue <u>can read</u> Ted's lips.
4. She also <u>uses</u> sign language.
5. They <u>had enjoyed</u> the evening.

10

The Subject and the Predicate

Every sentence has two parts. They are the *subject* and the *predicate*. The subject is what we are talking about. The predicate tells us something about the subject.

In this chapter, you will find the subject and the predicate in all kinds of sentences. Before you begin, do the Chapter Warm-Ups.

WARM-UP 1. Find the subject in each sentence. List the subjects on your paper. Study the examples.

In the morning Janet ate breakfast. — *Janet*
Stop it! — (*You*, understood)
Does your brother like tennis? — *your brother*
Mary's sister is in the class. — *Mary's sister*

1. Janet wanted a cassette recorder.
2. Her birthday was coming up soon.
3. On Saturday she looked at them in the store.
4. Her mother asked Janet a question.
5. "Would you like anything special for your birthday?"
6. "Please give me a cassette recorder."
7. April third is Janet's birthday.
8. She is an Aries.

■ **The predicate part of a sentence includes the verb and all of the words that tell something about the verb.**

All of the words that are not part of the subject are part of the predicate.

WARM-UP 2. Copy these sentences. Underline the predicate part of each sentence.

Examples: On Saturday Janet <u>went to the store.</u>
<u>Do</u> you <u>like music?</u>
An apple <u>is a good dessert.</u>

1. Many people know about their "sun sign."
2. Astrologers write daily horoscopes for the newspaper.
3. Janet is an Aries.
4. Harry Houdini, the magician, was also born under that sign.
5. The sign of Aries is a ram.
6. An Aries girl likes to be independent.
7. She will probably open her own doors!

■ **A subject and a predicate can both be compound. A sentence can also be compound.**

WARM-UP 3. Each sentence below contains a conjunction. Tell whether each sentence has a compound subject, a compound predicate, or whether it is a compound sentence.

1. Thomas Jefferson and Vincent Van Gogh were both Aries.
2. Janet is an Aries, but Darleen is a Gemini.
3. Gemini begins on May 22 and ends on June 21.

Now, you are ready to begin Lesson One.

LESSON ONE. THE SUBJECT OF THE SENTENCE

> The subject is the part of the sentence that tells what is being talked about. The main word in a subject is usually a noun or pronoun.

■ **The subject may be one word or many words.** Look at the examples below.

The French teacher gave the class homework.
She announced a quiz for Friday.
The man who taught us French last year moved to another town.

■ **The complete subject is usually made up of a noun or pronoun and all of the words that describe it.**

Some popular French songs were sung.

■ **The simple subject is the noun or pronoun.**

The _quiz_ on Friday was easy.
_We_ had to know five French verbs.
One _girl_ in the class had a perfect paper.

ACTIVITY 1. Copy the complete subject of each of these sentences on your paper. Circle the simple subject. A complete subject may be only one word.

1. Madame Donet teaches French.
2. The entire class speaks in French every day.
3. The teacher asks the students questions.
4. They must answer in French.
5. The students in the class must work hard.

■ **The simple subject cannot be the object of the preposition.** Look at these examples. The simple subject is underlined.

One of the girls was late.

Each of the students needs a book.

The prepositional phrase which describes the pronoun is part of the complete subject.

ACTIVITY 2. Find the simple subjects in these sentences. Write each one on your paper.

1. Each of the students wrote the answer on his paper.
2. All of my friends like music.
3. Yesterday eight of the students were absent.
4. All of them had the flu.
5. Two of the students had a fever.

■ **The subject of a sentence usually comes before the verb, but not always.** When a sentence begins with "Here" or "There," the subject comes after the verb. Look at the examples.

There will be _a bus_ at eleven-thirty.

Here is _your book._

ACTIVITY 3. Find the simple subjects in these sentences. Write each one on your paper.

1. There is a good program on TV tonight.
2. Here is the bus stop.
3. Here is the correct answer.
4. There is my school.
5. There are no more books about James Polk left in the library.

■ **In a question, the verb or part of the verb phrase may come before the subject.**

When *does* <u>Janet</u> *have* French?

Are <u>you</u> *leaving* soon?

■ **The interrogative pronoun may be the subject of a sentence that asks a question.** The subject in each sentence below is underlined.

<u>Who</u> is she?
<u>What</u> is happening?

ACTIVITY 4. Find the simple subject in each of these sentences.
1. Where will the meeting be?
2. What time will the meeting be?
3. What is happening at the meeting?
4. Will you be going to the meeting?
5. Has this group ever met before?

■ **In a command or a request, the subject is "you," even though the word "you" does not appear in the sentence.** The subject is "understood" to be the person we are speaking to. The subject is "you, understood." Look at the examples.

Please fix lunch soon.
(You) Please fix lunch soon.
Jack, stop bothering me.
Jack, (you) stop bother me.

ACTIVITY 5. Find the simple subject in each of these sentences.
1. Ted read the newspaper.
2. Read the newspaper.
3. Ted, read the newspaper.
4. Read the newspaper, Ted.
5. Please hurry!

■ **The subject of a sentence can be compound.** Here are two examples.

>*Janet and Sue* went to class.
>*The girl and her friend* went shopping.

ACTIVITY 6. Find the simple subjects in these sentences. Write them on your paper.

1. Neither Fred nor Alice went to the concert.
2. Both my hat and my gloves were lost.
3. Spring and summer are my favorite seasons.
4. Please bring my books to class.
5. Are my books or my papers in your locker?
6. There are not enough sodas and snacks for everyone.

LESSON REVIEW. Copy each of these sentences on your paper. Underline the complete subject. Then circle the simple subject.

1. Soon baseball season begins.
2. Will James be on the team?
3. He usually plays first base.
4. There will be a try-out on Friday.
5. Ted and Andy like to play baseball.
6. The college has a good team.
7. Most of last year's team graduated.
8. Where will the try-outs be?

LESSON TWO. THE PREDICATE

The predicate part of a sentence tells something about the subject. It always has a verb.

James <u>tried out for the baseball team</u>.

Andy <u>looks at new cars every weekend</u>.

ACTIVITY 1. Read these sentences. Copy only the predicate part of each sentence on your paper.

1. Sue's earring was lost yesterday.
2. She looked everywhere for it.
3. Darleen found it today.
4. One of the stones was missing.
5. Someone apparently stepped on it.
6. Sue walked home with Darleen.
7. Tiny greeted them with loud barks.
8. He tried to cheer up Sue.
9. The earrings had been her favorite jewelry.

■ **The main word in the predicate is the verb or verb phrase. The predicate also includes all of the words that tell something about the verb.**

ACTIVITY 2. Copy the predicate of each sentence on your paper. Circle the verb or verb phrase.

1. Mrs. Jones gave Janet a surprise birthday party.
2. Janet's brother, Ted, baked the cake.
3. Mr. Jones drove Janet to band practice that day.
4. Her friends came over and decorated the house.
5. Janet came home about six-thirty.
6. They all jumped out.
7. They screamed, "Surprise!"
8. The cake was delicious.
9. Everyone ate two pieces.
10. Ted was very pleased about that.

■ Any word that is not in the subject is in the predicate. Usually the predicate part of the sentence comes after the subject. Look at the example:

The whole family _enjoyed the party._

■ In a question, part of the predicate often comes before the subject. Look at these examples.

Did you _bring Janet a present?_

Where did you _put it?_

Was it _expensive?_

■ Adverbs and prepositional phrases which are used as adverbs may be at the beginning of the sentence. Look at the examples below.

At eleven o'clock everyone _went home._

Then Ted _ate the last piece of cake._

ACTIVITY 3. Copy only the predicate part of each of these sentences on your paper. Circle the verb or verb phrase.

1. Did Darleen bring Tiny to the party?
2. Why was Tiny left at home?
3. Maybe he didn't have a present.
4. After the party Darleen wrapped up a piece of cake to take home.
5. Was it for Tiny?
6. Tiny is only a dog.
7. He can't really expect a piece of cake.
8. At eleven-thirty Tiny heard Darleen's key in the door.
9. Usually he barks happily.
10. Tonight he was unusually quiet.
11. Then he saw the cake in Darleen's hand.
12. In an instant, that crazy poodle was barking happily.

■ **The predicate part of the sentence can be compound. A compound predicate has two verbs or verb phrases.**

The sun *moved behind the cloud and disappeared.*

The audience *clapped and cheered.*

ACTIVITY 4. Copy the predicate part of each of these sentences. Circle each verb or verb phrase.

1. Andy looked at new cars but didn't buy one.
2. The big cars cost too much and used too much gas.
3. The small cars got good gas mileage but were also expensive.
4. The used cars were often rusty and needed repairs.
5. Andy thought and thought but couldn't make a decision.

ACTIVITY 5. Write five sentences with compound predicates. Then circle each verb or verb phrase in your sentences.

■ Remember that the infinitive is *not* a part of the verb or verb phrase. It may be part of the predicate.

Verb   Infinitive

Janet <u>decided to leave early.</u>

ACTIVITY 6. Copy only the verb or verb phrase in each of these sentences.

1. Do you like to fish?
2. Howard wanted to know the answer.
3. Where do you like to go on vacation?
4. Sue's family likes to camp.
5. Tiny only likes to eat or bark.

LESSON REVIEW. Copy each of these sentences on your paper. Underline only the predicate part. Then circle the verb or verb phrase.

1. In the spring the weather gets warm.
2. People think about outdoor activities.
3. Some of the neighbors are planting flowers.
4. My neighbor George gets his fishing gear out.
5. I always know the first day of spring.
6. He is out in his yard with his fishing rod.
7. He likes to practice casting.
8. This year George plans to catch a huge fish.
9. He wants to catch the big one.
10. Last year it got away.
11. This year will be different.
12. He has already invited us to the fish fry.

LESSON THREE. COMPOUND SENTENCES

> A simple sentence is an *independent clause.* A *compound sentence* has two or more independent clauses joined together with a conjunction. Each clause has a subject and a predicate.

Subject   Predicate
Ted took his car to the garage, and

Subject   Predicate
the mechanic changed the oil.

■ **A compound sentence tells about two or more related events.**

Right: The mechanic fixed the car, and Ted drove it home.

Wrong: The mechanic changed the oil, and gas costs a lot these days.

ACTIVITY 1. Copy these sentences on your paper. Underline each subject once and each predicate twice.

1. After the party they were hungry; however, all of the restaurants were closed.

2. Alice has a cat, Mike has a gerbil, and Sandy has a hamster.

3. Mr. Jones likes sweets, but Mrs. Jones prefers fruit.

4. Andy wants to be a catcher, but Ted likes to play third base.

5. The new French teacher gives a lot of homework, but his tests are usually easy.

ACTIVITY 2. Write five compound sentences. Be sure the ideas are related. Punctuate them correctly.

■ Remember that a simple sentence may have a compound subject or a compound predicate. A compound sentence must have two or more complete sentences.

ACTIVITY 3. Number your paper from 1 to 5. Read these sentences. After each number write **Yes** if the sentence is compound. Write **No** if it is not.

1. Toyotas and Chevettes are small cars.
2. Andy is always looking at cars, but he hasn't bought one yet.
3. The telephone rang three times and then stopped.
4. The girls hurried, but they were late anyway.
5. After school we came home, ate dinner, did homework, and went to bed.

LESSON REVIEW. Copy each of these sentences on your paper. Underline the subject once and the predicate twice. Then decide whether the sentence is compound or not.

1. Andy counted his money and made a decision.
2. Most of the cars in town were too expensive, but one form of transportation was just right.
3. He needed something to drive to work, and he also needed something to drive to school.
4. Ted and Andy went to the showroom.
5. Andy's new "wheels" were there, and they looked great.
6. The motorcycle was not a fancy car, but Andy was happy!

CHAPTER REVIEW

Part 1. Copy each sentence on your paper. Underline the subject once and the predicate twice.

1. Everyone liked Andy's new motorcycle.
2. Darleen and Janet wanted a ride.
3. Andy gave Darleen a crash helmet.
4. She hopped on the back and smiled.
5. "Have you ever ridden on a bike before?"
6. She shook her head.
7. "Then this ride will be especially fun."
8. There was a small breeze that day.
9. They rode around the block and returned.
10. "Give me a turn!"

Part 2. Copy each sentence on your paper. Underline the subject once and the predicate twice. Then decide whether the sentence is compound or not.

1. The motorcycle took off, and Janet screamed.
2. "It is going too fast for me!"
3. Janet held on tightly, but she was still afraid.
4. Darleen and Ted stood on the curb and waited for Andy and Janet.
5. In a few minutes Andy pulled up, and Janet got off.
6. "That was fun, but I prefer a car."
7. Janet bent down and kissed the ground.
8. Ted just shook his head.

11

Four Sentence Patterns

In this chapter, you will 1) identify two kinds of verbs—transitive, and intransitive, and 2) identify four sentence patterns.

A verb that is *transitive* transfers the action to another person or thing. A sentence with a transitive verb must have a direct object. The object is a noun or pronoun.

Transitive
Verb   D.O.
Ted <u>*threw*</u> the ball.

A verb that is *intransitive* does not have an object.

Intransitive
Verb
The ball <u>*bounced.*</u>

Review the two kinds of verbs that you have already worked with in this book.

Action   — Andy <u>*bought*</u> a motorcycle.

Now, Andy <u>*has*</u> a motorcycle.

State-of-Being   — The motorcycle <u>*is*</u> new.

The motorcycle <u>*is*</u> at Andy's house.

■ **An action verb can be either transitive or intransitive. A state-of-being verb is always intransitive.**

First, look at some transitive verbs.

■ **A transitive verb transfers the action to another person or thing. A sentence with a transitive verb must have a direct object. The object is a noun or pronoun.** Look at the examples.

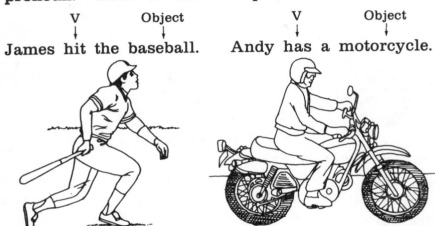

V   Object   V   Object

James hit the baseball.   Andy has a motorcycle.

WARM-UP 1. The transitive verb in each of these sentences is underlined. Find the direct objects and write them on your paper.

1. Last fall Janet's band <u>raised</u> money.
2. The band members <u>sold</u> Christmas cards.
3. The band <u>will enter</u> a national contest.
4. They <u>want</u> first place.
5. Janet <u>will play</u> a trumpet solo.

WARM-UP 2. Copy each of these sentences on your paper. Add a noun or pronoun that completes the thought. You may also add an adjective.

1. Every day Janet practices *her trumpet* .
2. Janet recently bought _____ .
3. The band director has _____ .
4. The band needs _____ .
5. The band director gave everyone _____ .

Now, look at some intransitive verbs.

■ **An intransitive verb does not have an object. The action is not transferred to a person or thing. The action expressed by an intransitive verb can be done by a person or a thing all alone!** Look at the examples.

Sue *is laughing.*   The fire burned.

■ **You may add adverbs or prepositional phrases which tell more about the action.** Look at the examples.

Sue laughed *happily.*
The fire burned *brightly.*
Janet walked *to the store.*

WARM-UP 3. Read these sentences. The verb in each sentence is underlined. Decide whether the verb is transitive or intransitive. Write your answers on your paper.

1. Janet is practicing her trumpet solo.
2. She has been practicing for an hour.
3. She is studying a new song.
4. Janet has been studying in her room.
5. Janet plays very well.
6. She plays the trumpet very well.

As you see, some verbs can be either transitive or intransitive. A transitive verb always has a direct object.

There are only a few basic sentence patterns in the English language. In this chapter you will study four of those patterns.

Pattern 1 has an intransitive verb. Sometimes you must add an adverb or prepositional phrase to express a complete idea.

<u>Example</u>: Sue *laughed.*
  (with V above *laughed*)

Pattern 2 has a transitive verb and a direct object. You may also add adverbs and prepositional phrases.

<u>Example</u>: Janet *has* a trumpet.
  (with V above *has* and D.O. above trumpet)

Pattern 3 has a transitive verb and a direct object. It also has an indirect object.

<u>Example</u>: She *gave* me a book.
  (with V above *gave*, I.O. above me, D.O. above book)

Pattern 4 has a transitive verb. It has a direct object. It also has an objective complement. The objective complement renames or describes the object.

<u>Example</u>: We *painted* the house red.
  (with V above *painted*, D.O. above house, O.C. above red)

WARM-UP 4. Look at the examples above. Try to identify the pattern of each of these sentences.

1. We gave John a new record.
2. The Rolling Stones made that record.
3. They made the record cover silver.
4. John listened to the record.
5. The book is on the shelf.
6. The band raised money for the trip.
7. Janet fixed everyone dinner.
8. We elected John president.

LESSON ONE. PATTERN 1 SENTENCES

In this lesson, you will study the simplest kind of sentence pattern. You need only a subject and a verb to express a complete thought. The verb in these sentences is *intransitive*.

An intransitive verb does not have an object. The action is not done *to* anyone or anything.

■ **Pattern 1 sentences contain an intransitive verb.** Look at the examples.

Pattern 1 Sentence: Subject — Verb

Sue *smiled.*   The sun *was shining.*

✗ ACTIVITY 1. Copy each of these sentences on your paper. Draw a line between the subject and the verb. Do yours like the example.

Tiny / was barking.

1. The band was playing.
2. The audience clapped.
3. Donna laughed.
4. The kitten purred.
5. She has been practicing.
6. They were singing.
7. I am listening.
8. My best friend moved.
9. The people on the next block are painting.
10. Dinner is burning!

■ **You can add an adverb to Pattern 1 sentences. The adverb answers a question about the verb. An adverb tells WHERE, HOW, or WHEN.** Look at the examples below.

The kitten purred *softly*.   Tiny barked *loudly*.

ACTIVITY 2.   Make two columns on your paper. In the first column, write the verb or verb phrase from each sentence.   In the second column, write the adverb.

Verb | Adverb

1. The fire is burning brightly.
2. Victor can run fast.
3. Sara is usually smiling.
4. Janet practices often.
5. I am reading now.
6. Nora is walking rapidly.
7. Yesterday it rained.

ACTIVITY 3.   The verbs in the list below are all intransitive.   Use each of them in a sentence.   Underline the subject once and the predicate twice.

1. go
2. walk
3. work
4. fall
5. live

6. laugh
7. scream
8. cry
9. inquire
10. think

■ A prepositional phrase may be added to the Pattern 1 sentence. The prepositional phrase may act like an adjective and describe the subject. It may act like an adverb and tell about the verb. Look at the example below.

Sue is walking to the store.

Sue is not doing anything **to** the store.
The phrase, *to the store*, tells us *where* she is walking.

ACTIVITY 4. Copy each sentence on your paper. Circle the verb. Then underline the prepositional phrase that tells about the action. Verb | Prep. Phrase

1. Everyone laughs at Tiny.
2. Karl is leaving for school.
3. Our neighbors moved to Ohio.
4. Mr. Jones works at the post office.
5. The book fell off the shelf.

■ **Review.** A Pattern 1 sentence:
   1. must have a subject and a verb.
   2. may have an adverb.
   3. may have a prepositional phrase.

ACTIVITY 5. Write ten Pattern 1 sentences on your paper. Your sentences may have an adverb or a prepositional phrase. The subject may not be doing anything to another person or another thing.

A Pattern 1 sentence may be a question. Part of the verb may be used to form the question. You may need to add a helping verb.

Statement — Tiny _is barking._

Question — _Is_ Tiny _barking?_

Statement — Sue _walked_ to the store.

Question — _Did_ Sue _walk_ to the store?

ACTIVITY 6. Read these sentences. Find the verbs and verb phrases. List each one on your paper.

1. Will Karl leave soon?
2. Which book fell off the shelf?
3. Where does Mr. Jones work?
4. Is Janet still practicing?
5. Are you listening to the radio?

ACTIVITY 7. See if you can recognize a Pattern 1 sentence. Here are ten sentences. Five of them follow Pattern 1. Number your paper from 1 to 10. Write _Yes_ after the number if the sentence follows Pattern 1. Write _No_ if it does not.

1. Janet's band is going to Florida.
2. The band will play for a large audience.
3. The band entered a contest.
4. Everyone has been practicing for weeks.
5. The band members are saving money.
6. They will go on a bus.
7. They will stay in a hotel in Miami.
8. Mrs. Jones told Janet to send her a postcard.
9. Ted wants a T-shirt.
10. Darleen bought a flute!

■ A Pattern 1 sentence may have a compound subject. Look at the example.

Sue and Darleen will leave soon.

■ A Pattern 1 sentence may have a compound predicate. Look at the example.

The band *will go to Florida and play.*

■ Two Pattern 1 sentences may be joined with a conjunction. Together, they will form a compound sentence. Look at the example.

Mrs. Jones laughed at the joke, *but* Mr. Jones only smiled.

ACTIVITY 8. Copy these sentences on your paper. Then do these things:

A. Find the complete subject or subjects. Underline them once.

B. Then, circle the simple subjects.

C. Next, find the complete predicate, or predicates. Underline them twice.

D. Then, circle the verbs or verb phrases.

These sentences will have a compound subject or a compound predicate. They may also be compound sentences!

1. The book and the pencil fell on the floor.
2. Janet laughed first and then cried.
3. Janet and the band are thinking about their trip and talking to each other.
4. Janet and Frank were on time, but they had to run down the hall.
5. Carol was reading in the morning, and she was writing in the afternoon.

ACTIVITY 9. Expand these Pattern 1 sentences by adding adverbs and prepositional phrases to the predicate. Do yours like the example.

Example — The girl walked.

Expanded sentence — The girl walked *quickly to the store.*

Add only adverbs or prepositional phrases!

1. The dog barked.
2. The fire burned.
3. The boys left.
4. Alice listened.
5. The lady laughed.

6. The man ate.
7. Snow fell.
8. We talked.
9. Bob is running.
10. His sister works.

ACTIVITY 10. Copy these sentences on your paper. Cross out the adverbs or prepositional phrases. Then copy the remaining words on your paper. Do yours like the example.

Example — The teacher listened ~~closely to the students.~~

Basic Sentence — The teacher listened.

1. The band played loudly at the dance.
2. Mrs. Jones left in a hurry.
3. Everyone laughed loudly at the joke.
4. Which student reported during first period?
5. Is Tiny barking at the cat now?
6. Several of the people cried during the movie.
7. Andy's motorcycle rides smoothly.
8. He inquired about the guarantee.
9. Are you leaving for school now?
10. Janet's band will go to Florida and play in a contest.

■ **A sentence diagram is a picture of a sentence that helps you see the parts of the sentence more clearly.** Study the rules for diagraming Pattern 1 sentences.

Rule 1.   Draw a horizontal line.
Divide it into two parts with a short vertical line.

Rule 2:   The word on the left is the simple subject (a noun or pronoun).
The word on the right is the simple predicate (a verb or verb phrase).

Example: Sue smiled.

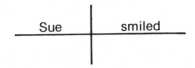

Rule 3:   Adjectives or prepositional phrases that describe the subject go under the subject.

Rule 4:   Adverbs or prepositional phrases that tell about the verb go under the verb.

Example: The small kitten purred softly.

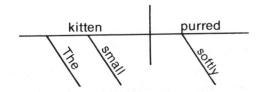

Example: The girl beside me laughed at Jim.

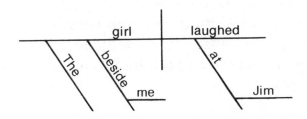

ACTIVITY 11. Diagram the five sentences below. Follow the rules on page 203. Be sure to draw your prepositional phrases like the example.

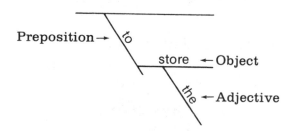

1. The school band went on a trip.
2. Janet went, too.
3. They went on a bus.
4. The band left in May.
5. The trip lasted for one week.

LESSON REVIEW. Copy each of these sentences on your paper. Underline the complete subject once and the complete predicate twice.

1. Which students are in the band room?
2. Everyone will ride on the bus.
3. Janet's trumpet fell on the floor.
4. Luckily it did not break.
5. Janet almost cried!
6. Janet is ready for the trip.
7. Everyone in the band is thinking about the trip.
8. Sue and Darleen are not going.
9. They will stay in school.
10. The band has been practicing and preparing for the trip for a long time.

LESSON TWO. PATTERN 2 SENTENCES

> A Pattern 2 sentence contains a transitive verb. A transitive verb has an object. The action is transferred to another person or thing. The object of the verb is a noun or a pronoun.

Pattern 2 Sentence: Subject — Verb — Direct Object

S   V   D.O.
Mrs. Jones bought a new *hat*.

S   V   D.O.
She has new *shoes* too.

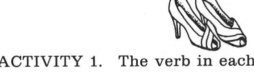

ACTIVITY 1. The verb in each of these sentences is underlined. Find the object and write it on your paper.

1. Len <u>found</u> the verbs.
2. He <u>wrote</u> them on his paper.
3. Then Len <u>located</u> the objects.
4. He <u>listed</u> them in order.
5. Len <u>raised</u> his hand.
6. I <u>have found</u> the answers to these questions.

ACTIVITY 2. Copy each of these sentences on your paper. Add a noun or pronoun that completes the thought.

1. Howard bought _____ .
2. We saw _____ .
3. For dinner we fixed _____ .
4. I bought _____ yesterday.
5. Have you ever studied _____ ?
6. Tiny lost _____ .

■ You know that the subject of a sentence is usually a noun or pronoun. The object of the verb is also a noun or pronoun.

Noun Used as Subject   — *Jane* baked a cake.

Noun Used as Object   — I saw *Jane*.

Notice that *Jane* is spelled the same in both sentences. Look what happens to the pronoun in the next examples.

Pronoun Used as Subject — *She* baked a cake.

Pronoun Used as Object   — I saw *her*.

Study the chart below.

FORMS OF PERSONAL PRONOUNS

Singular	Subject	Object
First person	I	me
Second person	you	you
Third person	he	him
	she	her
	it	it
Plural		
First person	we	us
Second person	you	you
Third person	they	them

ACTIVITY 3. Copy these sentences. Add the correct form of the pronoun in each space.

1. _____ wrote a letter. (I, Me)
2. Did you see _____ ? (he, him)
3. Fred found _____ in the library. (he, him)
4. Bill finally found _____ . (they, them)
5. _____ bought some new shoes. (She, Her)
6. _____ really liked that movie. (We, Us)

ACTIVITY 4. Across your paper write three headings: *Subject, Verb, Object.* Write the parts of the sentences below in the correct columns.

Subject	Verb	Object
My Aunt Alice	bought	a condominium.
She	fixed	her bicycle.

1. Sam received a letter.
2. The tabby cat caught a mouse.
3. I have been studying French.
4. The firefighters were climbing the ladders.
5. Mr. Jones loves that old song!
6. We cannot find her.

■ **The predicate of the Pattern 2 sentence must have a verb and an object. It may also have an adverb.**

  Adverb   V   D.O.
  Luckily Janet found her trumpet.

     V   D.O.   Adverb
  Andy bought a motorcycle *yesterday.*

  Adverb V D.O.
  I *just* found it.

ACTIVITY 5. Copy the complete predicate of each of these sentences on your paper. (HINT: Find the complete subject first. All of the words left over are in the predicate!)

1. Ted bought his tickets early.
2. You can diagram this sentence.
3. Tiny eats his dinner rapidly.
4. You can easily find the subject.
5. Yesterday Dan lost his notebook.
6. He found it today.

■ The predicate part of a Pattern 2 sentence may also have a prepositional phrase. Look at the example.

<pre>
            V   D.O.   Prepositional Phrase
</pre>
Janet found her trumpet in the band room.

■ The object of the verb is a noun. You may add adjectives and prepositional phrases that describe the object.

<pre>
        V   D.O.
</pre>
We baked a *chocolate* cake *with vanilla icing.*

ACTIVITY 6. Copy only the predicate part of each sentence. Then underline the verb and its object. Draw a circle around the prepositional phrase.

1. Janet wrote a letter to her uncle Albert.
2. My neighbors painted their house with bright colors.
3. Tiny wanted a new food dish for his birthday.
4. We filled the fish tank to the top.
5. Ted made pancakes for breakfast.
6. Sara found some blue shoes with white trim.

ACTIVITY 7. Write some Pattern 2 sentences. Each sentence must have a subject, a verb, and an object. You may also add adverbs and prepositional phrases. Here are some verbs to use.

1.	break	6.	dig
2.	bring	7.	freeze
3.	buy	8.	have
4.	catch	9.	spend
5.	choose	10.	take

You may use any tense in your sentences!

■ **Pattern 2 sentences may be questions. Remember that part of the verb is often placed before the subject to form a question.**

$$\text{V} \qquad \text{D.O.}$$
Statement — I <u>saw</u> a deer cross the road.

$$\text{V} \quad \text{V} \qquad \text{D.O.}$$
Question — <u>Did</u> I <u>see</u> a deer cross the road?

ACTIVITY 8. Find the verb or verb phrase and the object in each sentence. Write them on your paper.
1. The secretary typed a letter.
2. Is the secretary typing your letter?
3. Have you finished my letter yet?
4. Who is typing my letter?
5. Can you type my letter?
6. Has anyone seen my letter?

■ **Pattern 2 sentences may also be commands or requests. Remember that the subject of a command or request is always understood to be "you."** The word *you* may or may not appear.

$$\text{V} \qquad \text{D.O.}$$
Type my letter!

$$\text{V} \quad \text{D.O.}$$
Then mail it, please.

ACTIVITY 9. Copy each sentence on your paper. Circle the verb or verb phrase. Underline the object.
1. Take this book to the library.
2. Make a chocolate cake for dessert, please.
3. Finish your work at home.
4. Hang your coat in the closet.
5. Have another piece of chocolate cake!
6. Read these sentences carefully!

■ **A Pattern 2 sentence may have compound parts. You may join two Pattern 2 sentences together with a conjunction.**

Compound Verb — We <u>baked the cake</u> *and* <u>frosted it.</u>

Compound Object — We baked <u>a pie</u> *and* <u>a cake.</u>

Compound Sentence — <u>I found Paul,</u> *but* <u>he didn't have my books.</u>

ACTIVITY 10. Write five sentences for each kind described.

1. Pattern 2 with compound verbs.
2. Pattern 2 with compound objects.
3. Pattern 2 compound sentences.

ACTIVITY 11. Expand these Pattern 2 sentences by adding adverbs, adjectives, and prepositional phrases.

Example — We baked a cake.

Expanded — We baked a *chocolate* cake *in home economics class.*

1. Have you read that book?
2. Karl doesn't like that song.
3. Everyone enjoyed the party.
4. Wanda found Sharon in the lunchroom.
5. Carol can speak French.
6. Fix this car.
7. Please do your work.
8. Bring a main dish and a dessert.
9. Sue and Darleen bought shoes.
10. Ted has a part-time job; however, he also takes classes at the community college.

■ **Study these rules for diagraming Pattern 2 sentences.**

Rule 1: In a diagram, the object is placed on the base line. A short vertical line separates the verb and the object.

We baked cookies.

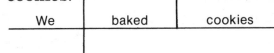

Rule 2: Put each adverb, adjective, or prepositional phrase under the word it is describing or telling about.

That man bought the last ticket to the show.

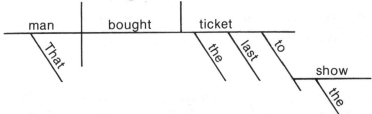

Rule 3: The understood subject of a command or a request is shown in parentheses.

Fix my car quickly.

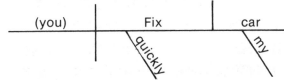

Rule 4: If the sentence is a question, change it into a statement. Then draw the diagram.

Did you find your coat?
You did find your coat.

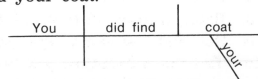

ACTIVITY 12.   Diagram these sentences. Look at the examples on page 211.   You may also want to look back on page 203.

1. Please stop that noise!
2. Jack left his book in his locker.
3. Have you seen Sally?
4. Darleen likes poetry by Edgar Allan Poe.
5. Mrs. Jones has blue eyes.
6. We bought a ticket for the early show.
7. He fixed the car quickly.

LESSON REVIEW

Part 1.   Find the direct object of the verb in each of these sentences.   List these words on your paper.

1. Howard asked several questions.
2. The teacher answered the questions.
3. Laura knows Sue very well.
4. Sue knows Darleen and Janet, too.
5. Have you seen that movie?
6. No, but I read the book.
7. Did you like it?
8. Yes, it had a good story.

Part 2.   Read these sentences.   Decide whether they follow Pattern 1 (intransitive verb) or Pattern 2 (transitive verb).   Write the number on your paper.

1. We met at three o'clock.
2. Janet met Darleen at three o'clock.
3. Will the band win the contest?
4. When are they leaving for Florida?
5. Please pack your suitcase tonight.
6. The bus leaves at five tomorrow morning.

LESSON THREE. PATTERN 3 SENTENCES

A Pattern 3 sentence has a transitive verb, a direct object, and an indirect object. The *indirect object* tells who will receive the direct object. An indirect object is a noun or pronoun that names the person receiving the direct object.

Pattern 3 Sentence:

Subject — Verb — Indirect Object — Direct Object

S   V   I.O.   D.O.

Mrs. Jones gave Janet a dollar.

Mrs. Jones gave the dollar.

(*Dollar* is the direct object)

Janet received the dollar.

(*Janet* is the indirect object.)

Important! A sentence cannot have an indirect object unless it has a direct object.

Important! The indirect object comes *before* the direct object in a sentence.

ACTIVITY 1. Read these sentences. Find the indirect objects and list them on your paper.

1. Darleen gave her mother a gift.
2. They gave Janet the prize.
3. The team awarded Jim the prize.
4. We asked her a question.
5. Darleen told Sue the answer.
6. Mr. Harris taught Ted math.
7. The bank lent Mr. Jones some money.
8. The salesclerk handed Janet the bill.
9. Andy allows himself a dollar for lunch.
10. Andy offered Ted his dessert.

■ **You may find the indirect object by rewriting the sentence. You may make the indirect object into a prepositional phrase.** Look at the example.

I.O.   D.O.

Andy offered *Ted* his dessert.

D.O.   Prep. Phrase

Andy offered his dessert *to Ted.*

ACTIVITY 2. Rewrite each of these sentences. Change the indirect object to a prepositional phrase.

Example: I bought *Mary* a gift.

         I bought a gift *for Mary.*

1. Darleen gave Tiny a bone.
2. Mrs. Jones paid the grocer twenty dollars.
3. Andy lent Ted his motorcycle.
4. Sue asked Janet a question.
5. The waitress served Sue and Janet lunch.
6. Mother bought Ted a gift.

ACTIVITY 3. Rewrite each of these sentences. Change the prepositional phrase to an indirect object.

Example: The postman handed her mail *to Mrs. Jones.*

         The postman handed *Mrs. Jones* her mail.

1. The teacher found a book for Janet.
2. Ted bought a new coat for himself.
3. Sue handed the note to Darleen.
4. Janet fixed lunch for herself.
5. The Academy gave the Oscar to the actor.

ACTIVITY 4. On your paper, draw a chart with four columns. Title the columns: *Subject, Verb, Indirect Object, Direct Object.* List the parts of these sentences in the correct columns.

Subject	Verb	Indirect Object	Direct Object
Mary	gave	me	a present

1. The director gave the band members their music.
2. Fred asked Mr. Smith a question.
3. The music company sent the school a bill.
4. Mr. Smith handed Janet her trumpet.
5. Mr. Smith offered the students his help.
6. The teacher gave the class homework.
7. Sue taught Darleen sign language.
8. Janet wrote her aunt a letter.
9. The school awarded Ted a scholarship.
10. Mr. Jackson gave Ted a raise.

ACTIVITY 5. Rearrange the words in each line. You will make a Pattern 3 sentence.

1. me told Sue secret a
2. made Ted cake Janet a
3. them served waitress dinner the
4. her a letter wrote Darleen aunt
5. gave bath Tiny Andy a
6. told team the coach play the the
7. a ribbon Tiny Darleen bought
8. herself snack fixed Janet a
9. me her sweater Janet lent
10. a him he handed dollar

■ **When the indirect object is a pronoun, it must be in the objective case.**

ACTIVITY 6. Copy each of these sentences on your paper. Fill in the correct form of the pronoun in the space.

1. __ gave Tom a message. (I, me)
2. Fred sent __ a letter. (he, him)
3. Martha told __ the answer. (she, her)
4. That teacher taught __ French. (we, us)
5. __ offered the lady our seats. (We, Us)
6. We served __ dinner. (they, them)

■ **To Pattern 3 sentences, you may add adjectives which describe the indirect object. You may also add prepositional phrases.**

Sentence   — I wrote my sister a letter.

Expanded Sentence — I wrote my *youngest* sister a letter.

Sentence   — She gave her friend a gift.

Expanded Sentence — She gave her friend *from Montana* a gift.

ACTIVITY 7. Read these sentences. The indirect object is underlined. Copy each sentence on your paper. Add an adjective or prepositional phrase that describes the indirect object.

1. Sally gave her <u>friend</u> a message.
2. Darleen offered the <u>lady</u> her seat.
3. The teacher told the <u>boy</u> the answer.
4. We made our <u>neighbor</u> an offer.
5. The newspaper boy brought the <u>people</u> their newspaper.

■ **Pattern 3 sentences can be questions. Part of the verb phrase may be placed before the subject. The question may also begin with an interrogative word.** Look at the examples.

I.O.
Will you *give* Ted a message?

I.O.
Who made me this chocolate cake?

ACTIVITY 8. Find the indirect objects in these sentences. List them on your paper.

1. Darleen, did you give Tiny his dinner?
2. Would you lend me your sweater for the evening?
3. Who asked Janet that question?
4. When did the teacher find Janet a book?
5. In what year did the Academy give John Wayne an Oscar for best actor?

■ **Pattern 3 sentences are often commands or requests.** Look at the examples.

Please send your uncle a letter.

Give me his new address.

ACTIVITY 9. Find the indirect objects in these sentences. List them on your paper.

1. Tell me the answer.
2. Please teach me Spanish.
3. Mom, bake us a cake for dessert tonight.
4. Tell me the truth.
5. Allow yourself enough time for breakfast.

■ **The indirect object can be compound.** Look at the example below.

I.O.
Fix your *father and his friend* some coffee.

I.O.
Will you give *Ted and Andy* a message?

ACTIVITY 10.   Copy each of these sentences on your paper. Add a compound indirect object in the space.

1. Write _____ a letter.
2. Give _____ more time.
3. Please tell _____ the answer.
4. Uncle Fred made _____ model airplanes.
5. Would you lend _____ five dollars?

■ **A Pattern 2 sentence has a direct object. A Pattern 3 sentence has an indirect object and a direct object.**

ACTIVITY 11.   Which of these are Pattern 3 sentences?   Which are Pattern 2?   Write the numbers on your paper.

1.   Have you read that book?
2.   Will you read me the book?
3.   Read the book to me.
4.   Bring your records to the party.
5.   Would you bring me a book from the library?
6.   Ted drove Andy to school yesterday.
7.   Could you drive me to school today?
8.   Victor made his mother a lamp at school.
9.   He also made a sewing box.
10.   Who made you that lovely sewing box?

■ **Study these examples for diagraming Pattern 3 sentences.**

In a diagram, the indirect object looks like a prepositional phrase. Put it under the verb.

Jack gave him a pencil.

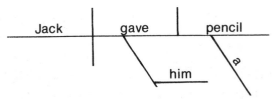

Here are examples of sentences with compounds.

Compound Subject

Janet and Sue laughed.

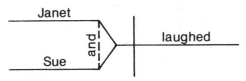

Compound Verb

They ran and ran.

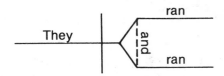

Compound Direct Object

Dan brought Ann and Meg.

Compound Indirect Object

Give Ted and me a ride.

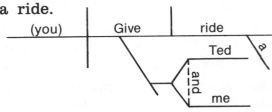

ACTIVITY 12. Diagram these sentences. Look at the examples on page 219. You may also want to look back on pages 203 and 211.

(All of these are Pattern 3 sentences.)

1. Please pass me the bread.
2. Jack lent Harry his car.
3. Jane made Yolanda an offer for her bike.
4. Lana wrote her married sister a letter.
5. Will you bring me some ice cream?

LESSON REVIEW

Part 1. Find the indirect objects in these sentences. List them on your paper.

1. Sue brought Darleen and Janet some books.
2. After dinner, Grandpa told the family some old stories.
3. Ted asked his grandfather a question.
4. Will you tell me the story about Dad again?
5. Allow yourself several hours for that report.

Part 2. Read each of these sentences. Decide whether it follows Pattern 1, Pattern 2, or Pattern 3. Write the number on your paper.

1. Janet and Ted like Grandfather's stories.
2. Tell us another one!
3. Grandfather tells very long stories.
4. They last for a long time.
5. Would you please fix me a soda and some ice cream?

LESSON FOUR. PATTERN 4 SENTENCES

> A Pattern 4 sentence has a transitive verb, a direct object, and an objective complement. A complement is a word that completes an idea. An *objective complement* is a noun or an adjective that completes the meaning of the direct object.

Pattern 4 Sentence:

$$\text{Subject} - \text{Verb} - \frac{\text{Direct}}{\text{Object}} - \frac{\text{Objective}}{\text{Complement}}$$

S   V   D.O.   Complement
The Smiths named their baby *Henry*.

(*Henry* renames the direct object. It is a noun.)

S   V   D.O.   Complement
The neighbors painted their house *blue*.

(*Blue* describes the direct object. It is an adjective.)

There are two words that sound exactly alike. They are *compliment* and *complement*. We are using the second word in this lesson.

Not this kind of compliment:

This is the meaning we need:

■ **The objective complement comes after the direct object in the sentence. It will be either a noun or an adjective.**

ACTIVITY 1. Find the objective complements in these sentences. List them on your paper.
1. The people elected George Washington president in 1788.
2. The frost turned the leaves many colors.
3. Happiness made the girl beautiful.
4. The police found the woman dead.
5. The dark room made us sleepy.
6. Everyone calls Laurence Olivier a great actor.
7. They made Mrs. Schwartz president of the company.
8. Andy considers Janet beautiful.
9. Are you making the cake sweet?
10. The hot sun turned the grass brown.

ACTIVITY 2. Add an objective complement to each of these groups of words. You may add either a noun or an adjective. Be sure your sentence makes sense. Write the sentence on your paper.
1. He found science class _____ .
2. The artist made the pictures _____ .
3. We elected Karl _____ .
4. Don't make the soup _____ .
5. They called him _____ .

ACTIVITY 3. Write five Pattern 4 sentences. Use the verbs below.
1. make or made
2. elect or elected
3. find or found
4. name or named
5. turn or turned

■ **Study the example for diagraming Pattern 4 sentences.**

In a diagram the objective complement goes on the base line. The objective complement is necessary to express a complete thought. Here is what the diagram looks like.

Janet dyed her blouse *red*.

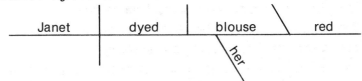

Important! The line before the objective complement (red) is slanted toward the direct object (blouse).

ACTIVITY 4. Diagram these sentences.

1. Andy found his computer class interesting.
2. His classmates elected Jack treasurer.
3. She made the pie spicy.
4. They named Mrs. Jones "Woman of the Year."
5. Janet painted her room purple.

LESSON REVIEW. Read these sentences. Find the objective complements. List them on your paper.

1. They named the young boy the winner.
2. We made Joe our leader.
3. Old age turned her hair silver.
4. They dyed the wool many colors.
5. You made that dinner too fattening!

CHAPTER REVIEW

Part 1. Transitive and Intransitive Verbs

Read each of these sentences. The verb is underlined. Decide whether the verb is transitive or intransitive.

1. One day Mr. Jones <u>bought</u> a computer.
2. He <u>called</u> it a microcomputer.
3. Micro <u>means</u> very small.
4. He <u>attached</u> the computer to the TV set.
5. The whole family <u>looked</u> at the computer.
6. <u>Can</u> we <u>use</u> it?
7. The computer <u>could show</u> video games.
8. Mrs. Jones <u>put</u> her recipe file on the computer.
9. They <u>used</u> it for their tax records.
10. That computer <u>ran</u> all evening!

Part 2. Sentence Patterns

Read each sentence below. Identify the sentence pattern it follows. Write the pattern number for each sentence.

Pattern 1 — Subject + Verb (adverb)
Pattern 2 — Subject + Verb + Direct Object
Pattern 3 — Subject + Verb + Indirect and Direct Objects
Pattern 4 — Subject + Verb + Direct Object + Objective Complement

1. We can do our math on the microcomputer.
2. It can add fast!
3. Andy and Ted asked the computer a question.
4. We should give the computer a name!
5. We will call it Einstein!

Part 3. Diagraming Sentences

Diagram the five sentences in Part 2.

Sentence Patterns
with a Linking Verb

> A *linking verb* is always a state-of-being verb. It does not express action. It is also intransitive. A linking verb cannot have a direct object.
>
> **Action verb** — James *plays* baseball.
>
> **Linking verb** — James *is* a baseball player.

In this chapter, you will recognize linking verbs. You will also study two more sentences patterns.

WARM-UP 1. The verb in each of these sentences is underlined. Decide whether it is an action verb or a linking verb. Write *Action* or *Linking* on your paper.

1. James <u>has</u> a new glove.
2. He <u>bought</u> the glove from Ted.
3. He <u>is</u> a good fielder.
4. James <u>is</u> also a good hitter.
5. James <u>likes</u> the new glove very much.
6. It <u>was</u> expensive.

■ **A linking verb joins the subject to a word in the predicate part of the sentence.**

Here are the two sentence patterns with linking verbs.

• Subject — Linking Verb — Adjective

• Subject — Linking Verb — Noun or Pronoun

Examples:

S   L.V. Adj.
Harry is tall.

S   L.V.   N
Harry is a student.

WARM-UP 2. Find the linking verbs in these sentences. List them on your paper.

1. Janet's Aunt Mary keeps active.
2. She is sixty years old.
3. Janet and Aunt Mary are good friends.
4. Aunt Mary is always happy.
5. She is Mr. Jones's sister.

■ **A subject and a linking verb do not express a complete thought by themselves. They need an adjective, a noun, or a pronoun to complete the idea.**

Not a sentence — The pudding tastes.
Sentence — The pudding tastes good.

WARM-UP 3. Find the adjective, noun, or pronoun that completes the thought in each sentence. List these words on your paper.

1. Sue seems friendly.
2. Sometimes she is shy.
3. She is a good student.
4. Darleen and Janet became friends with Sue.
5. Sue is a senior, also.

LESSON ONE. PATTERN 5 SENTENCES

> A Pattern 5 sentence has a subject, a linking verb, and a predicate adjective.

Pattern 5 Sentences:

Subject — Linking Verb — Adjective

Examples:

       S L.V.   Adj.   S. L.V.   Adj.

      The car is expensive. It looks great!

■ **The predicate adjective describes the subject in Pattern 5 sentences. This adjective is needed to complete the thought.**

ACTIVITY 1. Add an adjective that will complete each sentence. Copy the complete sentence on your paper.

1. Today the air feels _____ .
2. The sky looks _____ .
3. The day is _____ .
4. Everyone feels _____ .
5. They appear _____ .

■ **The linking verb is needed to help express the complete idea.**

Imagine that Ted wants to say something about his sister Janet.

The words, *"Janet pretty,"* do not express a complete thought. Ted needs a word to "link" his subject and the adjective that describes Janet. He needs a linking verb.

ACTIVITY 2. Add a linking verb to each of these groups of words. Write the sentence on your paper.

1. Lemons sour.
2. The sky blue.
3. Today warm.
4. James athletic.
5. Mrs. Jones serious.
6. The clouds fluffy.
7. Summer hot.
8. Mr. Jones friendly.
9. Janet pretty.
10. Sue shy.
11. The air chilly.
12. The motorcycle fun.

An adjective always describes a noun or pronoun.

■ **Adjectives may appear before nouns.**

My little sister is a *good* student.

Andy's new motorcycle was parked in front of *Janet's* house.

■ **Adjectives may appear after linking verbs.**

The weather is *sunny* and *mild* today.

■ When an adjective appears after a linking verb, it is describing the subject. This adjective is called a *predicate adjective.* It is in the predicate, but it describes the subject of the sentence.

ACTIVITY 3. Find all of the adjectives in these sentences. List them on your paper in order. Beside each one, write the noun or pronoun it is describing. Do yours like the example.

My brother is funny.   My — brother
                        funny — brother

1. New cars can be expensive.
2. That little boy looks hungry.
3. My youngest brother grows taller and taller.
4. The birthday cake was chocolate.
5. Tomorrow will be warm and sunny.

■ A Pattern 5 sentence has a subject, a linking verb, and an adjective. The adjective is in the predicate, but it describes the subject.

ACTIVITY 4. Make three columns on your paper. Title them *Subject, Linking Verb,* and *Adjective.* Read the sentences below. Write the parts of each sentence in the three columns. Do yours like the example.

Subject	Linking Verb	Adjective
Jim's report	was	interesting

1. The sunset was lovely.
2. My cousin is artistic.
3. The state of Florida is warm.
4. Rubik's cube is colorful.
5. The apartment is large.

■ You may add an adverb of degree to the Pattern 5 sentence. Adverbs of degree answer questions about adjectives.

S   L.V.   Adv.   Adj.

The day was *very* warm.

ACTIVITY 5. Find the predicate adjective in each of these sentences. Then add an adverb of degree.

Example: I feel good today.

               I feel *extremely* good today.

1. My grandmother keeps active.
2. She looks well.
3. She doesn't look old.
4. In fact, my grandmother looks young!
5. Grandma is spry for her age!

■ **You may also add an adverb or a prepositional phrase to answer questions about the verb.**

She is *always* busy *after school.*

HOW OFTEN?   always
WHEN?   after school

ACTIVITY 6.   Copy these sentences on your paper. Add adverbs or prepositional phrases that tell about the verbs.

1. Jim is tall.
2. Tiny is frisky.
3. That house is run-down.
4. The sky looks dark.
5. That painting is colorful.
6. Your salad is delicious.
7. Andy is active.
8. Ted seems quiet.
9. This motor sounds funny.
10. The notebook was neat.

ACTIVITY 7.   Find the basic sentence pattern in each of these sentences. Write it on your paper. Do yours like the example.

The park is usually empty after dark.

S   L.V. Adj.
The park is empty.

1. The month of June is usually pleasant.
2. The days grow longer then.
3. The air feels warmer in June.
4. Janet is especially happy about warm weather.
5. Tiny becomes friskier, too.

■ **The predicate adjective may be compound. Look at the example below.**

S   L.V.   Adj.
Jim's report was *short and funny.*

ACTIVITY 8. Copy these sentences on your paper. Complete them with compound predicate adjectives.

1. The new curtains were _____ and _____ .
2. Janet's speech will be _____ or _____ .
3. Andy's motorcycle is _____ but not _____ .
4. The month of May is _____ and _____ .
5. Usually after dinner Mr. Jones is _____ and _____ .

■ **You may combine two Pattern 5 sentences with a conjunction. You will have a compound sentence. Look at the example.**

S   L.V.   Adj.   S   L.V.
Mrs. Jones is usually serious, *but* Mr. Jones is

Adj.
more relaxed.

ACTIVITY 9. Combine Pattern 5 sentences to form four compound sentences. Use these conjunctions:

and   for   or   but

■ A Pattern 5 sentence may be a command or request. Look at the example.

Be quiet!

The imperative form of the verb "to be" is always "be." Remember that commands are always in the present tense.

ACTIVITY 10. Read each of these sentences. Copy only the linking verb and the predicate adjective on your paper. Do yours like the example.

Example: Keep quiet during my report!

Keep quiet.

1. Look friendly during the job interview.
2. Be nice to your teacher!
3. Be careful on that motorcycle.
4. Be ready for your class.
5. Remain loyal and true to your friends.

■ A Pattern 5 sentence may also be a question. Look at the examples.

Statement — Jim's report was short.
Question — Was Jim's report short?

Statement — May was warm this year.
Question — Was May warm this year?

ACTIVITY 11. Write five Pattern 5 sentences. Write them first as statements. Then write them again in question form. You will have ten sentences when you finish.

■ **Study these directions for diagraming Pattern 5 sentences.**

The predicate adjective is placed on the base line of the diagram. The adjective is necessary to have a complete thought. Because the adjective describes the subject, the line slants toward the subject.

The report was short.

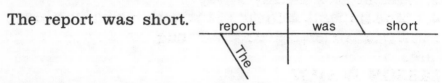

Diagraming adverbs of degree.

The adverb of degree tells you about the adjective. Place it under the adjective on a slanted line.

The pie was very hot.

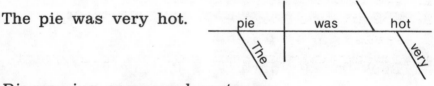

Diagraming compound sentences.

A compound sentence is two complete thoughts. Therefore, each sentence has its own base line. Join the two sentences together with a dotted line to show that they are connected.

Mrs. Jones is usually serious, but Mr. Jones is more relaxed.

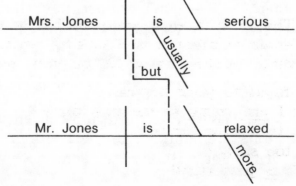

ACTIVITY 12. Diagram these Pattern 5 sentences. Be sure to place the correct words on the base line. Then place the adjectives, adverbs, and prepositional phrases correctly under those words.

1. Mike looks handsome in his new suit.
2. The chocolate pudding tastes good.
3. Dinner was finally ready.
4. Monday was windy, but it was warm outside.
5. William's report was too long.

LESSON REVIEW

Part 1. Find the linking verb in each sentence. Make a list of these verbs on your paper.

1. The lemon tasted sour.
2. Sue appears friendly.
3. James is very athletic.
4. Grandmother has been active for many years.

Part 2. Find the predicate adjectives in these sentences. List them on your paper.

1. That microcomputer is small but powerful.
2. Today the air feels chilly.
3. Everyone feels good today.
4. Be careful on that ladder!
5. Was my speech too long?

Part 3. The verb in each sentence below is underlined. Decide whether it is a linking verb or not a linking verb. Write *Yes* or *No* on your paper.

1. Stay loyal to your friends.
2. Later I am going to the movies.
3. Taste this stew for me.
4. Is it too salty?
5. No, it is just right!

LESSON TWO. PATTERN 6 SENTENCES

A Pattern 6 sentence has a subject, a linking verb, and a predicate noun or pronoun.

Pattern 6 Sentences:

Subject — Linking Verb — Noun or Pronoun

Examples:

    S   L.V.   P.N.   S   L.V.   P.N.
That building is a school. Janet is a student.

■ The *predicate noun or pronoun* always follows a linking verb. The predicate noun or pronoun renames the subject.

ACTIVITY 1. Copy these sentences on your paper. Complete each sentence with a predicate noun or pronoun.

1. In 1789, George Washington became _____ .

2. Aunt Marie is _____ .

3. The highest mountain in the world is _____ .

4. My favorite movie was _____ .

5. The capital of France is _____ .

■ Remember that adjectives describe nouns. There may be adjectives before the predicate noun. Look at the example.

S   L.V.   Adj.   P.N.
She is a pretty girl.

In the example above, _pretty_ describes girl.

ACTIVITY 2. Look at the adjective which is underlined in each of these sentences. Which noun or pronoun is each one describing?

1. George Washington was the first president.
2. My Aunt Marie is a good cook.
3. Carol is always friendly to me.
4. Ted looks tired today.
5. He seems over-worked.

■ The direct object can be a noun or a pronoun. Study the examples below to understand the difference between a direct object and a predicate noun or pronoun.

S   V   D.O.   S   L.V.   P.N.
Andy has a motorcycle.   Andy is a motorcyclist.

Motorcycle is not another name for Andy.

Motorcyclist is a person who rides a motorcycle. It renames Andy.

ACTIVITY 3. Look at the noun which is underlined in each sentence. Is it a direct object or a predicate noun? Write your answer on your paper.

1. James plays baseball in the spring.
2. He is the team captain.
3. Ken is the best catcher in the league.
4. He also hits the ball a mile.
5. Ken is the leading hitter on the team.

■ **You may add an adverb or a prepositional phrase to answer questions about the linking verb.**

James is <u>now</u> the team captain. (When?)

James is the captain <u>at our school</u>. (Where?)

■ **You may add a prepositional phrase to describe the predicate noun or pronoun.**

Agatha Christie was the author <u>of many books</u>.

ACTIVITY 4.   Find the predicate nouns or pronouns in these sentences.   List them on your paper. Remember, the predicate noun is not the object of the preposition.

1. Uruguay is a country in South America.

2. The Nile is one of the world's longest rivers.

3. Mars is the closest planet to the earth.

4. Coffee is a popular beverage in the United States.

5. *Gone With the Wind* was a popular movie in 1939.

6. Andy's favorite movie is still *Star Wars*.

7. Dawn has been Anne's best friend for two years.

ACTIVITY 5.   Write five Pattern 6 sentences.   Add as many adverbs, adjectives, and prepositional phrases as you want.   Label the required parts of the sentence. Do yours like the example.

      S   L.V.   P.N.
Jackie has been Cynthia's best friend for many years.

■ A Pattern 6 sentence may be a command or a request.

      L.V.   P.N.
Please be my friend.

         L.V.   P.N.
Always remain a true friend.

■ A Pattern 6 sentence may also be a question.

Statement — Carol and Don have been good friends.

Question — Have Carol and Don been good friends?

■ A Pattern 6 sentence may have compound parts. You may join two Pattern 6 sentences together with a conjunction.

  S   S   L.V.   P.N.
Tea and coffee are popular drinks.

         S   L.V. P.N.   P.N.
A nice dessert is cheese and fruit.

     S   L.V.   P.N.   S L.V.
John Adams was the president, but he was also

        P.N.
the vice-president.

ACTIVITY 6. Copy these sentences on your paper. Label the subject, the linking verb, and the predicate noun or pronoun.

1. Was Franklin Pierce a U.S. president?
2. Are those trees oaks or maples?
3. That small bird is either a wren or a finch.
4. Janet has been a student for thirteen years!
5. *The Good Earth* is a movie and a book.
6. Ted is a student and a salesclerk.

■ **Study these directions for diagraming Pattern 6 sentences.**

The predicate noun or pronoun is placed on the base line of the diagram. It is needed to express the complete thought The predicate noun renames the subject. The line is slanted toward the subject.

Mr. Ware is a Spanish teacher.

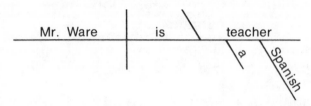

Here is an example of a compound predicate noun.

Ted is a student and a salesclerk.

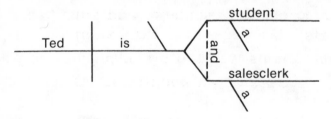

To diagram a question, change it to a statement. Then draw the diagram.

Is that an oak tree? That is an oak tree.

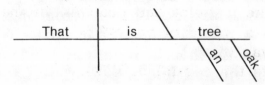

ACTIVITY 7. Diagram these Pattern 6 sentences.
1. Who is she?
2. Kim became our class secretary.
3. Sue and Darleen have become good friends.
4. Two popular sports are football and baseball.
5. Paul Dunbar was a poet, and he was a novelist.

LESSON REVIEW

Part 1. Find the linking verb in each of these sentences. Make a list of them on your paper.
1. *Romeo and Juliet* is a play by William Shakespeare.
2. Edgar Allan Poe was a poet and a story writer.
3. Warsaw is the capital of Poland.
4. Was that a flying saucer?
5. Aunt Marie has been the best cook in our family for years.

Part 2. Copy these sentences on your paper. Label the parts. Do yours like the examples.

S   L.V.   P.N.
Sudan is a country in Africa.

L.V.   S   Adj.
Is that ham too salty?

1. Two popular desserts are pie and cake.
2. The weather feels chilly today.
3. Always be true to your friends.
4. Jupiter is the largest planet in the solar system.
5. The lake is quiet and peaceful in the summer.
6. Is Dan a friend of yours?
7. Who was that?
8. Lima is the capital of Peru.

CHAPTER REVIEW

Part 1. Read each of these sentences. Find the verb and copy it on your paper. Decide whether it is a linking verb or not. Write *Yes* or *No* beside the verb.

1. Please taste this stew.
2. Is it too spicy?
3. No, it tastes just right.
4. Are you hungry?
5. No, I have already eaten dinner.
6. I am disappointed.
7. I fixed this stew especially for you.
8. Oh, I am sorry.
9. Do you want a small bowl?
10. OK, I will eat your stew!

Part 2. Read each of these sentences. Look at the underlined word. Is it a predicate adjective, a predicate noun, or a predicate pronoun? Write your answers on your paper.

1. Everyone is <u>happy</u> today.
2. Carol became a <u>cheerleader</u> this year.
3. He is a very good <u>lawyer</u>.
4. The capital of Egypt is <u>Cairo</u>.
5. Geography is an interesting <u>subject</u>.
6. John Steinbeck was a Nobel Prize <u>winner</u>.
7. That book is <u>one</u> of my favorites.
8. Who is <u>she</u>?
9. Of all the seasons, spring is my <u>favorite</u>.
10. Sue and Darleen will remain <u>friends</u>.

Chapter 13

Complex Sentences

Before you study complex sentences, review the meanings of three important terms.

A *word* is a set of letters that has meaning.

A *phrase* is a group of words that are working together. For example:

Prepositional Phrase — across the road

Verb Phrase — has been

A *clause* is a group of words with a subject and a predicate (or verb). There are two kinds of clauses: independent clauses (sentences), and dependent clauses. For example:

Independent Clause — James walked home.

Dependent Clause — Because he missed the bus.

WARM-UP 1. Look at these groups of words. Which are phrases? Which are clauses? Write the answers.

1. Over the river.
2. If he leaves.
3. Will have been late.
4. The youngest girl in school.
5. Whoever wants an apple.

■ An independent clause is a sentence. It expresses a complete thought.

■ A dependent clause has a subject and a verb, but it is not a sentence. There are three kinds of dependent clauses.

Adverb Clause —
$$\overset{S}{James}\; \overset{V}{laughed}\; \underline{\overset{S}{when}\; \overset{V}{he}\; \overset{}{heard}}$$
$$\underline{\overset{D.O.}{the\; joke.}}$$

Noun Clause —
$$\overset{S}{I}\; \overset{V}{remember}\; \underline{\overset{S}{what}\; \overset{V}{she}\; \overset{}{said.}}$$

Adjective Clause —
$$\overset{V}{There}\; \overset{S}{is}\; \overset{}{the}\; \overset{}{lady}\; \underline{\overset{S}{that}\; \overset{V}{I}\; \overset{}{paid.}}$$

WARM-UP 2. Read these sentences. Find the dependent clauses. Copy them on your paper.

1. That is the boy who just joined the team.
2. The girl who won the contest is in my class.
3. Janet will study until she finishes.
4. Before the game began, the team exercised.
5. A prize will be given to whoever finished first.

■ The dependent clause is introduced by either a subordinating conjunction or a relative pronoun.

Subordinating conjunctions: *because, if, when, since*

Relative pronouns: *that, which, who, whoever, what*

WARM-UP 3. Find the word that introduces the dependent clause in each sentence. Write it on your paper.

1. Because Shelly was late, she missed the bus.
2. I will fix dinner if you are hungry.
3. Janet hoped that the band would win first place.
4. James admires the man who coaches his team.
5. What Darleen said was not clear to everyone.

■ **Sentences may be grouped according to purpose, or according to pattern.**

WARM-UP 4. Copy each of these sentences on your paper. Label the parts. Write the purpose of the sentence on your paper. Do yours like the example.

     S   V   D.O.

  Darleen is reading a good book. — Statement

1. Shelly missed the bus.
2. Will James hit a home run today?
3. Paint the house green.

■ **Sentences may also be grouped according to structure. A sentence is either simple, compound, complex, or compound-complex.**

Simple (One subject and one predicate):

    Sue went to school.

Compound (Two or more sentences joined with a conjunction):

    We looked at new cars, but they were expensive.

Complex (One independent and one dependent clause):

    If the rain stops, we can begin practice.

Compound-Complex (Two independent clauses and at least one dependent clause):

    After I met the girl who moved next door, we became friends; but the next year she moved.

WARM-UP 5. Identify the type of each sentence below according to structure. Write your answers.

1. They practiced hard and won the game.
2. I'd like to go, but I am too tired.
3. Because we were late, we hurried; but we missed the train anyway.
4. I'll drive if you are too tired.

LESSON ONE. THE ADVERB CLAUSE

A clause is a group of words with a subject and a verb. An adverb clause is used in a sentence exactly like an adverb. It tells something about the verb. Look at the examples below.

Adverb   — James went home *early.*

Adverb Phrase— James went home *after school.*

Adverb Clause— James went home *when practice was over.*

The adverb, the adverb phrase, and the adverb clause each tell WHEN James went home.

■ Adverbs also answer the questions, WHERE? HOW MUCH? WHY? HOW OFTEN? HOW SOON? Look at the examples below. The adverb clauses are underlined.

WHERE?   Darleen was happy *wherever she went.*

HOW MUCH?   James gave *as much as he could.*

WHY?   Janet is in the band *because she likes music.*

HOW OFTEN?   Janet practices *whenever she has time.*

HOW SOON?   *When practice is over,* James will go home.

ACTIVITY 1.   Find the adverb clause in each of these sentences. Copy it on your paper.

1. James likes to jog whenever he can.
2. If he gets up early, he jogs in the morning.
3. James jogs because he enjoys it.
4. Unless it is raining hard, he jogs every day.

■ **Remember that a clause must have a subject and a verb.**

The example below is a simple sentence with an adverb **phrase**. The phrase has no subject or verb.

S   V   D.O.   Prep.   N
Janet has French *before lunch.*

Adverb Phrase

The example below is a complex sentence with an adverb **clause**. The subject of the clause is *James*. The verb is *arrived*.

S   V   S   V
Darleen waited an hour *before James arrived.*

Adverb Clause

ACTIVITY 2. Read each of these sentences carefully. Find the subject and the verb of each clause. Decide whether it is a simple sentence or a complex sentence. Write the answers on your paper.

Examples:

S   V   S   V
The team was behind until James hit a home run.
— Complex

S   V
Practice lasted until noon. — Simple

1. Every afternoon the baseball team practiced.
2. When practice is over, the players are tired.
3. The team begins with warm-up exercises.
4. If they don't warm up well, injuries are likely.
5. Sometimes the team practices on Saturdays.
6. When it rains, the team can't practice.
7. Baseball is not usually played in the rain.

■ An adverb clause may also answer questions about another adverb. These clauses are adverbs of degree. They answer questions like HOW MUCH? or HOW FAR?

S   V   D.O.   S   V

James hits the ball farther *than anyone can.*

The adverb clause tells HOW MUCH farther James can hit the ball.

■ Sometimes part of the clause is missing. We say the missing part is "understood."

S   V   D.O.   S

James hits the ball farther *than anyone.*

In the incomplete clause the verb is missing. The verb is "understood" to be *can.*

■ An adverb clause may also answer questions about an adjective. These clauses are also adverbs of degree. Sometimes part of the clause is also understood. Look at the examples.

Complete Clause — Sam is taller than the others are.

Incomplete Clause— Sam is taller than the others.

The adverb clause tells HOW MUCH taller Sam is.

ACTIVITY 3. Copy these sentences on your paper. Underline the adverb clauses.
1. Tiny can bark louder than any other dog.
2. Janet practices longer than anyone else does.
3. Is Darleen taller than Sue?
4. James jogged longer than the others.
5. Charlotte is as pretty as she can be!

LESSON REVIEW

Part 1. Copy these sentences on your paper. Underline the dependent clauses.

1. Sue has been deaf since she was born.
2. Because Darleen became Sue's friend, she learned sign language.
3. Anyone can learn sign language if he tries.
4. Sometimes sign language is easier than English is.
5. Darleen uses sign language when she is with Sue.

Part 2. Copy each sentence on your paper. Draw one line under the subject in each clause. Draw two lines under the verb in each clause. Write any "understood" words in parentheses.

1. We will go to the beach when summer arrives.
2. Andy bought a motorcycle because he needed transportation.
3. Get some rest if you are tired.
4. No one can run faster than James.
5. James can hit the ball farther than anyone on the team can.

Part 3. Read these sentences. Look for the subject and verb of each clause. Tell whether each sentence is simple or complex.

Reminder: A simple sentence has one independent clause.

A complex sentence also has a dependent clause.

1. Darleen and Sue went to the baseball game.
2. They wondered if the team would play.
3. The field was wet because of the rain.
4. They smiled when they saw the team on the field.
5. Although the field was wet, the game began.

LESSON TWO. THE NOUN CLAUSE

> A clause is a group of words with a subject and a verb. A *noun clause* is used in a sentence exactly like a noun. Look at the examples below.

Subject
     S   L.V.   Adj.
— *What Janet said* was not clear.

Predicate
Noun
    S   L.V.   P.N.
— That book is *what I need*.

Direct
Object
   S   V   D.O.
— I remember *what you said*.

Object of
Preposition
    S   V   D.O.   O.P.
— Mrs. Jones fixed dinner for *whoever was hungry*.

■ Each noun clause has its own subject and verb. It may have a direct object or a predicate noun. The clause may be any of the six sentence patterns. Look at the example.

   S   L.V.   P.A.
Whoever is ready should begin first.

Whoever is ready names the person that is the subject of the sentence. Because it is a clause, it has its own subject, verb, and predicate adjective.

ACTIVITY 1. Read each of these sentences. Find the noun clause and write it on your paper. Then decide what part of the sentence the entire clause is.

1. The teacher said that my answer was wrong.
2. Janet wondered what Darleen would say.
3. Who will be first has not been decided.
4. They argued about who should go first.
5. This is what I want.
6. Ted knows what the score is.

■ **The noun clause is introduced in a sentence by a relative pronoun.** Some common relative pronouns are listed below.

that	who (subject)
what	whom (object)
whatever	whose (possessive)
whichever	whoever (subject)
	whomever (object)

■ **The relative pronoun is part of the sentence pattern of the noun clause.** Look at the examples.

D.O.　　S　　V
I remember *whom you called.*

S　　V　　D.O.
I remember *who called me.*

P.N.　S　L.V.
I remember *who you are.*

The pronoun *that* and *what* have only one form. They do not change when they are subjects or objects. The pronoun *who* does change, however. You must know what the sentence pattern of the noun clause is before you can decide whether to use *who* or *whom*.

ACTIVITY 2. Read these sentences. Decide whether *who* or *whom* should be used in each sentence. Write the sentences correctly on your paper.

1. I know ___ called you. (who, whom)
2. I know ___ you are. (who, whom)
3. I know ___ you saw yesterday. (who, whom)
4. I know ___ you invited to the dance. (who, whom)
5. I know for ___ you bought that gift. (who, whom)

■ We often use the relative pronoun "that" to introduce a noun clause. Sometimes we choose to leave it out of the sentence. Either way is correct. Look at the examples.

Do you think *that* he is nice?

Do you think he is nice?

■ The other relative pronouns cannot be left out. Look at the examples.

Correct: Did you hear *what* I said?

Wrong: Did you hear I said?

ACTIVITY 3.   Copy each of these sentences on your paper. Underline the noun clause. Circle the relative pronoun. (The relative pronoun *that* may have been left out of the sentence. Put it in and circle it.)

1. Do you know who found my book?
2. Yes, Janet found the book you lost.
3. What I need right now is that book!
4. I am offering a reward to whoever finds my book.
5. Do you think Janet has my book now?

ACTIVITY 4.   The noun clauses in these sentences are underlined. What part of the sentence pattern is each one?

What I said was not important. — Subject

1. I have a book for whoever wants it.
2. I knew that I would be late.
3. Some ice cream is what I need right now!
4. What you see is what you get!
5. Tell me what the answer is.

■ **An appositive is a noun or a noun clause.**

An appositive explains another noun in the same sentence. Look at each example below. The appositive is underlined. The noun which is explained by the appositive is in bold print.

My **friend** _Darleen_ has a dog.

Tiny, _a French poodle,_ belongs to Darleen.

The **idea** _that Tiny can protect her_ is silly!

ACTIVITY 5. Find the appositive in each sentence. List the appositives on your paper. Beside each one write the noun which the appositive is explaining.

1. Do you know who wrote this line: "All the world's a stage"?
2. Fred's hope that he would win the race kept him going.
3. People laughed at Columbus's idea that the world was round.
4. The nineteenth constitutional amendment, which gave women the right to vote, changed history.
5. Herbert Hoover, the thirty-first president, was an engineer.
6. Galileo's discovery that the earth revolved around the sun changed scientific thought.
7. A bibliography, which is a list of books, appeared at the end of the report.

LESSON REVIEW. Copy these sentences on your paper. Underline the noun clauses. What part of the sentence is each clause?

Example:

Did you hear <u>what she said?</u> — Direct Object

Sue knew <u>that she and Darleen were friends</u> —
Direct Object

1. We went shopping for whatever we needed.
2. I think that you can diagram this sentence.
3. The idea that love conquers all is lofty.
4. A glass of lemonade is what I need.
5. She said she's tired.
6. When the paper is due is not clear.
7. Where he was going was not known.
8. I know where he was going.
9. That map is what he needs.
10. He went on an errand for whoever asked him.
11. People laughed at Tom's belief that he could win the contest.
12. You get what you pay for.
13. Is this what Tiny brought home?
14. Andy forgot where he put his book.
15. Tell me who is coming.
16. How Sue did the job was important.

Try to figure this one out. If you can, you've got it!

What she will do next no one knows.

LESSON THREE. THE ADJECTIVE CLAUSE

> An adjective is a word that describes a noun or pronoun. An *adjective clause* is used in a sentence exactly like an adjective. Look at the examples below.

Adjective — The <u>middle</u> girl is my sister.

Adjective Phrase — The girl <u>in the middle</u> is my sister.

Adjective Clause — The girl <u>who is in the middle</u> is my sister.

■ You can express the same idea in all three ways. Each sentence is correct. Notice that the adjective clause follows the noun or pronoun.

More examples:

The book *that I gave him* was expensive.

Are you the one *whom I met at the party*?

Jim invited Sandy, *who is the prettiest girl in school*.

The lady *whom I recommended* got the job.

ACTIVITY 1. Find the adjective clause in each of these sentences. Copy it on your paper.

1. A girl whom I know won first prize in a contest.
2. The look that Janet gave Ted was meant to kill!
3. The answer which she gave was wrong.
4. The boy who sits in the first seat is absent.
5. We bought a new refrigerator which is guaranteed for one year.

■ An adjective clause is introduced by a relative pronoun. Some common relative pronouns are: *who, whom, whose, which, what,* and *that.*

ACTIVITY 2. Read these sentences. Find the adjective clause in each one. Copy it on your paper. Circle the relative pronoun.

1. The band that Janet belongs to went to Florida.
2. They entered a contest that someone organized for high school bands.
3. The director of the band, whose name is Mr. Smith, was very pleased.
4. The band which he had trained performed very well.
5. Mr. Smith hoped that the band which he directed would win first place.

ACTIVITY 3. In each of the sentences below, an adjective is underlined. Rewrite the sentence. Change the adjective to an adjective clause.

Example: Janet's band went to Florida.

The band that Janet belongs to went to Florida.

1. An old bus took the band to Florida.
2. The band had a wonderful trip.
3. They stayed in a small hotel.
4. Everyone enjoyed the warm weather.
5. They all looked forward to an exciting contest.

LESSON REVIEW

Part 1. Copy these sentences on your paper. Underline the adjective clauses. Then write the noun or pronoun each is describing.

Example:

Spring is the season <u>that I like best.</u> — season

1. Please get potato chips that come in a box.
2. Did you know the people who gave the party?
3. Mike is the one who plays right field.
4. The man who drove the bus was very nice.
5. The dress that Sue wore to the party was blue.
6. The girl who was in line behind me bought the last tickets.
7. The man who lived next door moved to Florida.
8. Sue's favorite actor was the one who starred in that movie.
9. James read a book which was about the Civil War.
10. We rented a new apartment which had three bedrooms.

Part 2. Read each of these sentences carefully. Decide whether it is simple, compound, or complex. Write your answers on your paper.

1. I'd like to help you; however, I am too busy.
2. Do you know what Ted said?
3. I think that I've seen that movie before.
4. The person in the middle of the line is my brother Ted.
5. Andy said he was hungry.

LESSON FOUR. COMPLEX AND COMPOUND-COMPLEX SENTENCES

A compound sentence has two independent clauses.

I would drive, but I am too tired.

A complex sentence has one independent clause and one dependent clause.

I will drive *if you are tired.*

A compound-complex sentence has two independent clauses and one or more dependent clauses.

I will drive *if you are too tired,* but it is your decision.

ACTIVITY 1. Read each of these sentences carefully. Find the independent and dependent clauses. Decide whether the sentence is compound, complex, or compound-complex.

1. After she graduates, Janet hopes to find a summer job.
2. She asked Ted about a job in Mr. Jackson's store, but he said Mr. Jackson was not hiring.
3. Janet was discouraged, but she kept on looking.
4. Janet knows that there is a job for her somewhere!
5. Janet is a girl who doesn't give up easily, and she will look until she finds a job.

■ **When you want to know how a sentence is constructed, you analyze it.**

To *analyze* means to break something down into its parts. You must analyze a sentence to find out whether it is compound, complex, or compound-complex.

ACTIVITY 2. Read the sentence in the box. It is a riddle. It is also a compound-complex sentence. Then follow the directions below.

> If you remove my skin,
> I will not cry,
> but you will.

1. Find the first independent clause. Write it on your paper and label the parts.

2. Now find the coordinating conjunction. It connects two independent clauses. Write it on your paper.

3. Find the second independent clause. Write it on your paper. Label the parts.

4. Now find the subordinating conjunction. It introduces an adverb clause. Write it on your paper.

5. Next find the dependent (adverb) clause. Write it on your paper. Label the parts.

6. Read the riddle again. What is it?

■ **A complex sentence may have more than one dependent clause.** Look at the example below.

Adjective Clause

Richard Wright, <u>who was born on a plantation,</u>

worked as a dishwasher

Adverb Clause

<u>before he became the author of *Native*

Son.</u>

ACTIVITY 3. Answer these questions about the sentence shown above.

1. What is the independent clause in the sentence? Write it on your paper.

2. What is the subject of the independent clause?

3. What is the verb of the independent clause?

4. Is the verb transitive or intransitive?

5. What are the parts of speech of the words in the phrase "as a dishwasher"?

6. What noun is the adjective clause describing?

7. What question does the adverb clause answer?

8. What is the subject and the verb of the adjective clause?

9. What is the subject and the verb of the adverb clause?

10. There are three verbs (or verb phrases) in the sentence. Which one is a linking verb? What word completes the thought in that clause?

■ **The same idea may be expressed in different kinds of sentences.**

Compound — Ted is a student, but he also has a part-time job.

Complex — Ted, who is a student, also has a part-time job.

Compound-
Complex — Ted is a student, but he is also a person who has a part-time job.

ACTIVITY 4. Look at the three examples above. Read these questions. Answer them on your paper.

1. Which sentence expresses the idea best?
2. What is the independent clause in the second example? Write it on your paper.
3. What kind of dependent clause is "who is a student" in the second example? Is it a noun, adjective, or adverb clause?

ACTIVITY 5. Rewrite each of these sentences or pairs of sentences.

Example: Ted needs a map, and here it is.
Here is the map that Ted needs. (or)
The map that Ted needs is here.

1. Summer has arrived, and we will go to the beach.
2. Gallaudet College is in Washington, D.C., and Sue wants to go there.
3. Graduation will be in June. Ted and Andy will go to see the girls graduate.
4. The fish are biting, and we will go to the lake.

Now, go back and analyze your sentences. What kind of sentence is each one?

ACTIVITY 6. Read each of the sentences below. Find the independent and dependent clauses. Decide what kind of sentence each one is. Tell whether it is complex or compound-complex. Analyze the sentence pattern of each clause.

Example: If James gets a scholarship, he knows that he can go to college.

Step 1.   The independent clause is "he knows that he can go to college."

Step 2.   There is a noun clause which is the direct object of the independent clause: "that he can go to college."

Step 3.   "If James gets a scholarship" is an adverb clause.

Step 4.   This is a compound-complex sentence.

Step 5.   These are the sentence patterns of the clauses:

S   V   D.O.
If James gets a scholarship

S   V   D.O.
he knows (that he can go to college)

S   V   Prep. Phrase
that he can go to college.

1. Mr. and Mrs. Jones play golf when the weather is warm.
2. Mr. Jones hits the ball farther than Mrs. Jones can, but he doesn't putt well.
3. "A new putter is what I need."
4. Mrs. Jones, whose clubs are old, plays golf very well.
5. Both of them know that new clubs would not really help!

■ **Direct and indirect quotations are noun clauses.**
Look at the examples.

S	V	Direct Object

Mrs. Jones said, "I enjoyed our golf game."

S	V	Direct Object

Mrs. Jones said that she enjoyed golf.

ACTIVITY 7. Change each of these indirect quotations to direct quotations. Punctuate your quotation like the example above.

1. Mr. Jones told Mrs. Jones that he wants a new putter.
2. He reminded her that his birthday was in June.
3. She told him that she would buy him a putter.
4. Mr. Jones said that he wanted to play golf again soon.
5. Mr. Jones said that he would win next time!

LESSON REVIEW. Analyze each of these sentences. Decide whether it is simple, compound, complex, or compound-complex. Write your answers on your paper.

1. Mrs. Jones planned a party for Janet because she was graduating from high school.
2. She invited Darleen, Sue, Andy, and James.
3. She told Mr. Jones that she wanted to buy Janet a car, but he said it was too expensive.
4. "Janet has a part-time job, and she can save her money for a car."
5. "Buy her a watch instead," Mr. Jones said.

CHAPTER REVIEW

Part 1. A clause always has a subject and a verb. Look at these groups of words. Which are clauses? Which are phrases? Write the answers on your paper.

1. Who is coming
2. to the party
3. for Janet?
4. Mrs. Jones is planning a party
5. because Janet is graduating
6. from high school.
7. It is sad to leave good friends
8. after so many years.

Part 2. The dependent clauses in these sentences are underlined. You must decide whether each clause is an adjective, adverb, or a noun. Write your answers on your paper.

1. The person who is planning the party for Janet is her mother, but Mr. Jones has said that he will help.
2. Ted, who has already graduated, has gotten Janet a present which he purchased at Mr. Jackson's store.
3. The party will be held after the graduation exercises are over.
4. Mrs. Jones has planned a surprise for whichever guest arrives first.
5. Whoever it is will be surprised.
6. Because the party is for Janet, the guests will not expect a gift.
7. Mrs. Jones will prepare plenty of food because she knows that everyone will be hungry.

Part 3. Read the sentence in the box below. Then follow the directions and answer the questions. Write your answers on your paper.

> The gift that Mrs. Jones bought for the first guest is a record album.

1. Find the independent clause in the sentence. Write it on your paper.
2. Label the parts of the independent clause.
3. Write the dependent clause on your paper.
4. Label the parts of the dependent clause.
5. Is the dependent clause an adjective, an adverb, or a noun?
6. What kind of sentence is it? Is it compound, complex, or compound-complex?
7. What is the purpose of the sentence? Is it a statement, a question, or a command?

Part 4. Read each of these sentences carefully. Analyze the sentence. Then decide whether it is simple, compound, complex, or compound-complex. Write the answers on your paper.

1. Here is a riddle.
2. What has a tongue, but it does not talk?
3. You tie them up when you go for a walk.
4. I'm sure that you know the answer to the riddle, and I want you to write the answer on your paper beside the number 5.
5. Write the answer to the riddle on your paper.

Chapter 14

Verbals and Verbal Phrases

> A *verbal* is a verb that we use as another part of speech. The three kinds of verbals are infinitives, gerunds, and participles.

■ An **infinitive** is *to* + a verb. Usually we use it as a noun, but it may also be an adverb or an adjective.

> I like *to swim.* (Noun)
> He practices *to win.* (Adverb)
> We had lots of food *to eat.* (Adjective)

■ A **gerund** is a verb that ends in *-ing* and is used as a noun.

> *Swimming* is good exercise. (Subject)
> We enjoy *swimming.* (Direct object)

■ A **participle** is a verb form that we use as an adjective. There are present and past participles.

> The doll is *lost.* (Past)
> The *barking* dog scared the stranger. (Present)

WARM-UP 1. Find the verbals in these sentences. List them on your paper.

1. The smiling child was opening presents.
2. Speed is important in running.
3. Jack likes to read.
4. The new magazine was torn.
5. They decided to buy a new house.

■ **Because an infinitive, a gerund, and a participle are verbs, they may have complements. They may also have adverbs.** Look at the examples.

Infinitive Phrase — He hoped *to win the contest.*

Gerund Phrase — *Cooking dinner* was fun.

Participial Phrase — We saw Ted *walking down the street.*

WARM-UP 2. Find the verbal phrases in these sentences. List them on your paper. Identify the kind of verbal each phrase is.

Ted plans *to leave early.* (Infinitive Phrase)

1. Darleen hoped to find a job.
2. After winning the contest, the band celebrated.
3. Their celebrating lasted a long time.
4. To be a good musician takes a lot of practice.
5. In Hanover, James went to play baseball.
6. Winning the games was important to James.
7. He hoped to win a scholarship.
8. James saw the coach standing on the field.

In this chapter, you will find verbals and verbal phrases. Now you are ready to begin the lessons.

LESSON ONE. INFINITIVES AND INFINITIVE PHRASES

An infinitive is *to* + a verb. Look at the examples in these sentences.

Andy and Ted decided *to go* to the lake.
Their plan was *to leave* early.
They hoped *to catch* many fish.

■ An infinitive is usually in the present tense. It can also be in the present perfect tense. Look at the examples in the sentences below.

They decided *to be gone* by six o'clock.
They hoped *to have caught* ten fish by noon.

ACTIVITY 1. Find the infinitives in these sentences. List them on your paper.

1. Andy found someone with a small boat that they wanted to use.
2. Andy and Ted really like to fish.
3. They planned to catch enough fish for dinner.
4. Mrs. Jones agreed to fry the fish.
5. She also decided to make cole slaw and french fries.
6. Andy and Ted were on the lake by seven o'clock, ready to make their first cast.

■ **Be sure that you do not mix up infinitives with prepositional phrases.** Look at the examples.

	V
Infinitive	— The boys like *to fish.*
Prepositional Phrase	— They went *to the lake.* (N)

An infinitive is *to* + a **verb**.

The prepositional phrase is *to* + a **noun**.

ACTIVITY 2. Look at the underlined phrases. Copy them on your paper in order. Identify each phrase as an infinitive or a prepositional phrase. Do yours like the example below.

> They went to the lake to fish
>
> to the lake — Prepositional phrase
>
> to fish — Infinitive

1. When Andy and Ted got to the lake, they saw other people ready to fish.

2. They carried their equipment to the boat.

3. Soon they were ready to begin.

4. "I will try to catch the first fish," Ted said.

5. "Do you really hope to beat the champion?" Andy said to Ted.

6. "I hope to have caught at least one big one by ten o'clock," said Ted.

7. They said hello to the other boaters.

8. "Look!" Andy pointed to another boat.

9. "That man just started to reel in his line."

10. "He will need a big pan to fry that fish!"

■ **Remember that an infinitive is a verb, but it may be used as a noun, an adverb, or an adjective in a sentence.** Look at the examples.

D.O.
Ted wants *to catch* a big fish.
(What does Ted want?)

Adverb
He will need a big pan *to fry* his fish.
(Why does he need a big pan?)

Adjective
Andy had plenty of bait *to use*.
(What kind of bait does Andy have?)

■ **You must look at the sentence pattern to figure out how an infinitive is used in a sentence.**

ACTIVITY 3.   The infinitives in the sentences below are underlined.   Copy them on your paper.   Decide whether each infinitive is a noun, an adverb, or an adjective.   Remember that subjects, predicate nouns, direct objects, and objects of prepositions are nouns.

1. To catch a big fish was Ted's ambition.
2. His greatest hope was to catch a big fish.
3. After an hour, they decided to move to another spot.
4. Their attempts to catch a fish were unsuccessful.
5. They tried and tried to catch some fish.
6. These fish are hard to catch.
7. "A fish would be fun to catch!"
8. "Hey! I am about to catch a fish!"

An *infinitive phrase* is an infinitive plus any adverb, adverb phrase, or complement it may have.

■ **An infinitive is a verb form. It may have an adverb or adverb phrase to answer questions about its action.** Look at the example below.

To leave early was the plan.

To leave is an infinitive. It is the subject. *Early* is an adverb. It answers the question WHEN?

■ **An infinitive may also have a complement. It may have a direct object or a predicate noun.** Look at the examples.

We wanted to join the club.

Club in the direct object of the infinitive.

He wanted to be the president.

President is the predicate noun. The infinitive *to be* is a linking verb.

■ **The infinitive may also have a predicate adjective.** Look at the example.

We wanted the dinner to taste good.

Good is a predicate adjective. *To taste* is a linking verb. The infinitive *to taste* is an objective complement. Objective complements are explained in Chapter 11, Lesson Four.

ACTIVITY 4. Find the infinitive phrase in each sentence. Copy it on your paper. Do yours like the examples.

<pre>   INF.   D.O.
Examples: I am about to catch a fish!</pre>

<pre>   INF. D.O. ADV. PHR.
           Ted wanted to reel it into the boat.</pre>

"Into the boat" is a prepositional phrase. It is used as an adverb. It answers the question WHERE?

1. Ted began to reel the fish into the boat.
2. The fish started to fight hard.
3. The fish struggled to get free from the hook.
4. Ted was about to bring it into the boat.
5. Andy got a net to help him.
6. To land that fish was their goal.

■ **Sometimes the preposition "to" is missing from the infinitive.** Look at the example below.

"Don't make me laugh," shouted Andy.

ACTIVITY 5. Find the verb of each sentence. Then find the infinitive. Write the infinitive on your paper.

1. Will you let me help you?
2. They heard the other boaters cheer for Ted.
3. "Let me see that fish," they all said.
4. They watched Ted hold his fish high in the air.
5. Their attention made Ted smile.

ACTIVITY 6. Find the infinitives in these sentences. List them on your paper. After each infinitive, write how it is used in the sentence.

1. Andy's turn to catch a fish came soon.
2. He began to reel his fish to the boat.
3. The fish tried to get free.
4. It seemed to pull hard.
5. To catch a fish is not easy.

LESSON REVIEW. Read each of these sentences. Find the infinitive phrase. Copy it on your paper.

Example: It seemed to pull hard.

    to pull hard

1. Andy and Ted wanted to be home by dark.
2. They decided to stop at six o'clock.
3. Andy began to count the fish.
4. They had hoped to catch many fish.
5. To catch enough fish for dinner had been their goal.
6. "How many fish are big enough to eat?" asked Ted.
7. "We have enough to feed your family and mine," answered Andy.
8. "Mom will need a big pan to fry this one," Ted said.
9. "Let's get ready to go home," Andy said.
10. They were both ready to leave. It had been a good day.

LESSON TWO. GERUNDS AND GERUND PHRASES

> A *gerund* is a verb that ends in *-ing*. It is always used as a noun. We use gerunds in sentences in the same ways that we use nouns. Look at the examples.

Subject — *Drinking* and *driving* do not mix.

Direct Object — The dog began *barking*.

Predicate Noun — My favorite sport is *swimming*.

Object of a Preposition — The student got in trouble for *cheating*.

Appositive — Andy enjoys two things: *fishing* and *riding* his motorcycle.

ACTIVITY 1. Find the gerund in each sentence. Write it on your paper.

A *gerund phrase* is a gerund plus any adjective, adverb, prepositional phrase, or complement it may have.

■ A gerund is a verb form. We use it in a sentence as if it were a noun. A noun may have an adjective that describes it. Look at the example.

I get in trouble for *loud barking.*

Loud describes the gerund *barking.*

■ A gerund may also have an adverb or adverb phrase. Look at the example.

I like *jogging in the morning.*

In the morning tells us WHEN James likes jogging.

■ Because a gerund is a verb. it may have complements. Look at these examples.

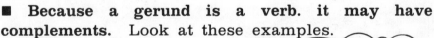

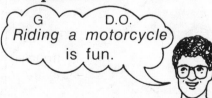

G   D.O.
Riding a motorcycle is fun.

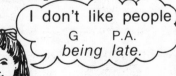

I don't like people
G   P.A.
being late.

Motorcycle is the direct object of the gerund *riding.*

Late is a predicate adjective. *Being* is a linking verb.

ACTIVITY 2. Find the gerund phrase in each of these sentences. Copy it on your paper. Identify the part the gerund plays in the sentence. Do yours like the example.

Example: Getting ready for school is the worst part of the day.

Getting ready for school — Subject

1. James watched the running of the Boston Marathon on television.
2. Winning that race was one of his dreams.
3. He began thinking about it when he was very young.
4. He got an idea for having his own marathon in Hanover.
5. He began finding joggers.
6. Setting up the race was easy.
7. James enjoys two things: running and winning!

■ **Don't confuse progressive verbs with gerunds.** Look at the example.

Verb Phrase — James *was running* early every day.

Gerund — James likes *running* every day.

ACTIVITY 3. Use each of these words or phrases in a sentence. Use it correctly!

Verb Phrases	Gerunds
1. will be starting	4. being
2. is beginning	5. finding
3. were going	6. running

LESSON REVIEW. Read these sentences. Find the gerunds or gerund phrases. List them on your paper.

Example: My hobby is collecting stamps.
collecting stamps

1. Flying an airplane seems exciting.
2. Reading books is a way to relax.
3. We enjoyed swimming in the lake.
4. An architect earns his salary by planning buildings.
5. Tiny always gets in trouble for chasing cats.
6. The singing and dancing were good in that play.
7. I like cooking, but not cleaning up.
8. Finding gerunds is easy.
9. Locating a needle in a haystack is usually difficult.
10. A farmer earns money by growing food.
11. Knowing you has been my pleasure!
12. Some people like weeding their gardens.
13. Planning our vacation was fun.
14. His favorite sport is fishing for trout.
15. Janet's hobby is reading.

LESSON THREE. PARTICIPLES AND PARTICIPIAL PHRASES

> A *participle* is another verb form. Participles are used in sentences as adjectives. We also use them as part of a verb phrase. Look at the examples.
>
> **Verb Phrase** — The deer *was running* through the woods.
>
> **Participle** — The *running* deer was beautiful.

ACTIVITY 1. Look at the underlined words. Decide whether they are part of the verb or whether they are participles. Do yours like the example.

The <u>barking</u> dog scared the child. — Adjective
The dog was <u>barking</u> at the child. — Verb

1. Your cold is probably <u>catching</u>.
2. We are <u>leaving</u> early in the morning.
3. We will be <u>catching</u> the train.
4. The girl came <u>running</u> to the train.
5. The <u>howling</u> wind kept us awake all night.
6. The wind was <u>howling</u> all night.

■ A participial phrase is a participle plus an adverb or an adverb phrase. It must be next to the noun or pronoun it is describing.

(Running at full speed,) she caught the bus.

The participial phrase describes *she*.

■ The participle may also be in the past tense.

Potato chips are the only snack (needed for the party.)

Needed for the party describes *snack*.

ACTIVITY 2. Copy these sentences on your paper. Underline each participial phrase. Draw a line to the noun or pronoun it is describing.

1. Howling wildly, the wind frightened the child.
2. Janet lent her book to the girl sitting in the first row.
3. Expecting the worst, Ted was pleasantly surprised with his grade.
4. The keys locked inside the car were of little use.
5. Reading her book intently, Mrs. Jones did not hear Ted enter the room.
6. Mr. Jones mailed the letter addressed to the bank.
7. Recommended by his teachers, James was offered a scholarship.
8. Dinner cooked by Janet was a special treat for Mrs. Jones.
9. To Darleen, looking from the top of the building, the people looked like ants.

ACTIVITY 3. Find the participles and participial phrases in these sentences. Write each one on your paper. Then write the word which it describes.

Example: Running at full speed, the girl caught the bus.

Running at full speed — girl

1. Walking to school, we passed a new apartment building.
2. Speaking in front of the class, James got nervous.
3. Sodas are the only thing needed for the party.
4. Lost kittens are pitiful.
5. Swimming at the beach, we were frightened by a shark.

LESSON REVIEW. Read each of these sentences. Find the participle or the participial phrase. Write it on your paper.

1. We could see the boy running around the track.
2. The old man found his lost dog.
3. Rowing rapidly, we soon crossed the river.
4. The broken bike could not be fixed.
5. Standing on the corner, we watched the cars go by.
6. Arriving early, we were first in line for tickets.

CHAPTER REVIEW

Part 1. Find the verbals in these sentences. List them on your paper. Identify each one as either an infinitive, a gerund, or a participle.

1. To Janet, graduating from high school was an exciting event.
2. Ted went to the graduation to see Janet.
3. Smiling from the stage, Sue received her diploma.
4. James, walking across the stage, almost tripped.
5. "I am a little bit sorry to leave good old Wilson High School," said Darleen.
6. "It's a good excuse to have a party," Andy laughed.

Part 2. Find the verbal phrases in these sentences. List each one on your paper. Identify each one as either an infinitive, a gerund, or a participial phrase.

1. Standing in front of the school for a last look, the girls had tears in their eyes.
2. "Graduating from high school is something that you will always remember," said Mrs. Jones.
3. As they drove away, Sue turned to catch a last look at her school.
4. Shutting her eyes, Sue thought that she would always remember the good friends that she had made.
5. They all met at Janet's house to celebrate the graduation.

See how well you understand sentence patterns!

MASTERY TESTS FOR PART TWO

MASTERY TEST 1. Read each group of words. Decide whether it is a phrase or a clause. Remember that a clause has a subject and a verb.

1. Janet and Ted
2. thought about the year
3. that had just passed.
4. It had been a good year.
5. Both Janet and Ted
6. had been to Florida.
7. They had had good times.
8. that they would always remember.
9. Next year Janet and Ted
10. would both be in college,
11. but they would still be at home
12. with their parents.
13. Sue and James were both going away,
14. but they would be home for vacations.
15. Because Darleen had decided to work,
16. she would still be around
17. which made Janet glad.
18. They could also count on Andy,
19. who would be a sophomore,
20. to come by on his motorcycle!

MASTERY TEST 2. Copy the sentences below and identify the sentence parts. Do yours like the examples:

          S   V   D.O.   O.C.
The neighbor painted his house green.

          S   L.V. P.A.   P.P.
Grammar is easy for me.

Use the abbreviations in the box.

S	Subject	O.C.	Objective Complement
V	Action Verb	P.A.	Predicate Adjective
L.V.	Linking Verb	P.N.	Predicate Noun
D.O.	Direct Object	P.P.	Prepositional Phrase
I.O.	Indirect Object		

You do not need to identify an adjective unless it is the complement of a linking verb.

1. Sue went to Gallaudet College.
2. James won a scholarship.
3. He would play football for the college.
4. The college gave James a scholarship.
5. James was a good athlete.
6. Darleen was excited about her new job.
7. The new job made Darleen happy.
8. Only Tiny was not doing anything special!

MASTERY TEST 3. Read each of these sentences. Decide whether it is simple, compound, complex, or compound-complex. Write the answer.

1. Janet, Darleen, and Sue had enjoyed high school.
2. They knew that their lives would be different now, but they looked forward to the new year.
3. They would all be together during vacations, and they would write letters while they were separated.
4. Ted and Andy would still go to Hanover Community College.
5. Ted would drive his car, and Andy would ride his motorcycle.
6. They all hoped that James would be successful at college.

MASTERY TEST 4. Find the verbals in these sentences and copy them on your paper. Beside each one write *Infinitive, Participle,* or *Gerund.*

Example: Because her cooking was excellent, she hoped to win the cooking contest.

    cooking — Gerund
    to win — Infinitive
    cooking — Participle

1. Mr. Jones was home watching television.
2. He enjoys relaxing after a busy day.
3. Janet had gone to her room to do her homework.
4. They heard someone knocking at the door.
5. Darleen had come to tell Janet about her job.
6. "Working in a busy office is fun," she told Mr. Jones.
7. "I am glad to see that our children are doing so well," said Mrs. Jones.

Index